FORGE EQUIPPING

A FIELD MANUAL FOR THE KINGDOM LABORERSHIP MOVEMENT

FORGE

Forge Equipping: A Field Manual for the Kingdom Laborership Movement

© 2023 by Forge. All rights reserved.
Published by Forge, 14485 East Evans Avenue,
Denver, Colorado 80014

ISBN 979-8-9854126-7-3 (paperback)

Created by Forge.

Visit us online at www.forgeforward.org

CONTENTS

MAKE EXTRAORDINARY IMPACT

Did you know that you are God's Plan A to spread His love to everyone around you? This is the calling of a Kingdom Laborer.

It doesn't matter how old you are, where you live, or what you do—God created you to make an extraordinary impact.

Every day you are surrounded by hundreds of people in your sphere of influence. Even in small, ordinary moments, you can show them the powerful love of Jesus.

We are here to help you forge forward as a Kingdom Laborer.

Igniting Hearts on Fire and Lives on Purpose

Forge challenges people to make spiritual decisions and embrace a vibrant, intimate relationship with Jesus.

Through that relationship, they activate their God-given purpose to live whole-heartedly and intentionally for Jesus every day.

Advancing the Kingdom. Every day. Everywhere.

God is using Forge to raise up Kingdom Laborers: people who love God, love others, and advance the Kingdom everywhere they go.

The Mission in Action

Forge comes alongside churches, ministries, and individuals to challenge and equip people to make spiritual decisions and activate their God-given purpose.

Forge creates global and multi-generational impact through dynamic preaching, practical equipping, and discipleship resources.

- Proclaiming Repentance and Revival
- Championing Intimacy with God
- Equipping People for Thier God-Given Mission
- Mobilizing Disciples of All Nations
- Raising Up More Kingdom Laborers

Welcome to the Forge Laborership Movement!

FORGE EQUIPPING ORIENTATION

You will get out of this experience what you choose to invest. Enter in with an open and learning posture. Step into places that push and surpass your comfort level.

- Participate!

- Ask Questions.

- Trust God!

- Engage the spiritual battle. Stand against the enemy and fight for the work God is doing! It may not be easy, but it is worth it.

- Submit to leaders. Trust them. They are for you.

- Listen! We're all adults.

- You're on a "need to know" schedule. Trust it.

- Please be punctual. When we have a break it is important that you stay within hearing distance. Don't wander off—time is tight, and we need everyone in the right place at the right time.

- Please actively clean up after yourself, and look out for your teammates. Help one another keep our learning spaces and meal spaces clean.

Basic Daily Schedule

- 6:00 am: Wake up—workout, shower, breakfast, personal devotions. If you are someone who wants to be sure to get workouts in during the summer, mornings are your time to accomplish this!
- Here, there, and everywhere
- 11:00 pm: Curfew—in your rooms

Relationships

- Don't wait to go deep with your team. Engage early!
- No dating. Always be above reproach in your interactions.
- No one-on-one, private conversations with the opposite gender—be where people can see you.
- No guys in girls' rooms or girls in guys' rooms—meet in public spaces.

Disconnect—what does it look like for you to be present and available this summer?

- TV, Computers, Phones
- If it has an "on-off" button, best to leave it "off."

Be aware of others.

- Hotel rooms—remember you have neighbors.
- Surroundings—we're a big team and will have a large presence wherever we go.
- Service
- Humility

Health

- Drink water!
- Communicate if you're not feeling well.
- Sleep
- Activity (some planned)

Media

- #ForgingLives
- TheForgeApp.com *

includes Spiritual Life Notebook, Scripture Memory, Multiplying Movements, and other resources.

Forge Equipping Field Manual

- Take note of the structure of this journal. It is a tool for you to keep with you for long after your time at Forge Equipping.
- Take good notes.
- Engage each teaching to the fullest.
- Notice the "Engage the Message" section in each chapter after the empty note taking pages. This is a great place for you to decide on some key personal takeaways for each message.

OVERVIEW VISION

Matthew 9:35-38

Jesus' Prayer Request:

Ask the Lord to send more laborers into the harvest field. Will you become the answer to Jesus' prayer request?

"Abide in me, and I in you. As the branch cannot bear fruit by itself, unless it abides in the vine, neither can you, unless you abide in me" (John 15:4 ESV)

For you, God, tested us; you refined us like silver" (Psalm 66:10 NIV)

To become a Kingdom Building Laborer, you must get up close to God, the Forge.

A Kingdom Laborer is someone who loves God, loves others, and advances the Kingdom wherever they go, every day, everywhere!

DAILY LIFE OF A KINGDOM LABORER: KINGDOM VALUES

DEEP VALUES | LOVING GOD

1. Loving God Intimately
   Matthew 22:34–40

2. Seeking His Kingdom Always
   Matthew 6:33

3. Being Directed by His Spirit Daily
   Galatians 5:16–26
   John 10:27

4. Living Passionately for Christ
   Romans 5:1–5
   Acts 5:41-42

5. Continual Transformation through the Holy Spirit
   2 Corinthians 3:18
   Luke 24:15, 32
   Hebrews 4:12

6. Engaging in the Spiritual Battle
   James 4:7
   2 Corinthians 10:3–6
   Ephesians 6:10–17

7. Growing Together with Other Believers
   Ephesians 4:11–16
   I John 1:7
   Proverbs 27:17

WIDE VALUES | LOVING PEOPLE

1. Loving All People
   Matthew 22:34–40

2. Participating in the Priesthood of Believers
   I Peter 2:9

3. Engaging in the Ordinary
   Matthew 9:10
   and many other accounts of Jesus' ministry

4. Spiritually Multiplying through One-at-a-time Reproduction
   2 Timothy 2:2
   Titus 2:3–8
   Matthew 28:16–20

5. Fulfilling the Great Commission as Your Ultimate Purpose
   Matthew 28: 16–20
   Mark 16:15

6. Living in Unity with All Believers
   John 17:23

7. Living a Life of Transformational Impact
   I Corinthians 3:10–15
   Acts 5:12–16
   John 15:16

BECOMING A KINGDOM LABORER: LIFE CHANGE WHEEL

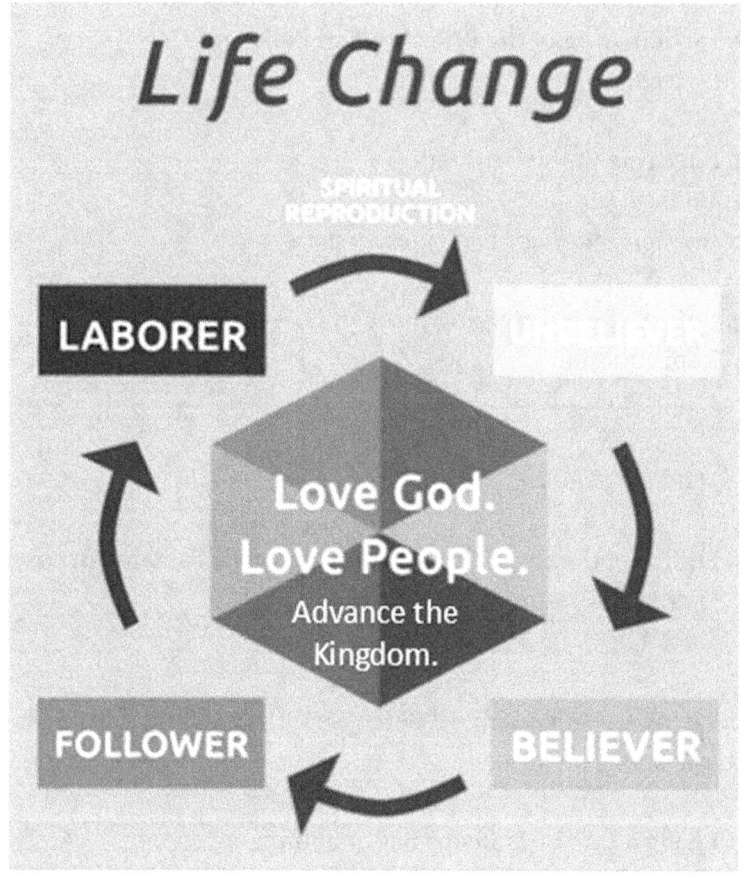

SCRIPTURE CHALLENGE

We whole heartedly believe in the importance of scripture memory. As part of your training, we encourage you to engage with scripture memory.

1. What scripture will you be memorizing? (Perhaps 3-10 verses)

2. Consider writing out the scripture here, by hand, to begin the process of memorization:

_____

_____

_____

_____

_____

_____

_____

_____

_____

_____

_____

_____

_____

_____

_____

_____

TIPS FOR SCRIPTURE MEMORY

- Make it bite size. Try to memorize small sections at a time

- Engage memorization every day. Each day build on what you memorized the day before.

- Consider memorizing just before taking a nap or sleeping for the night, this can help solidify the words in your mind.

- Make a flash card with the scripture reference on the front and the verse(s) on the back. Cary it around in your pocket. Go through your memory verses when you have free time. You might also use a phone app for this.

Keep it up! Memorizing God's word becomes a blessing for you and those around you as you are able to draw on His Word at a moment's notice.

MY LIFE STORY

Write out bullet points for the main overview of your life.
Capture your most significant moments, both positive and
negative. What impacted you most? What changed the direction
of your life? What made you become who you are today? How
has God shown up in your life?

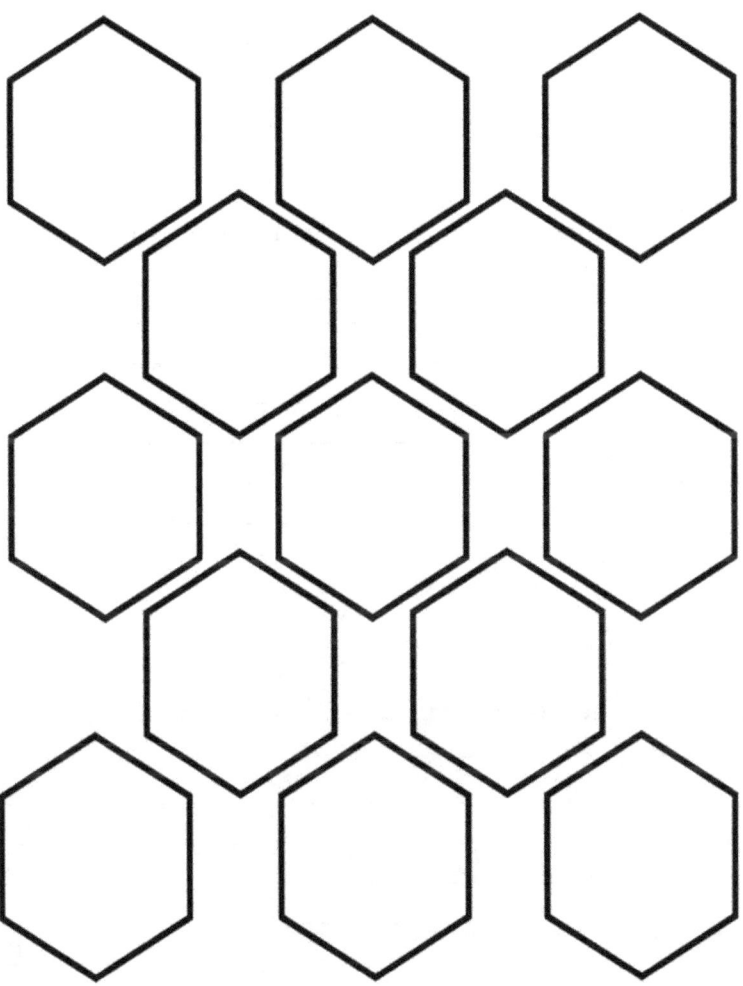

ENGAGING THE MESSAGE

1. What are your top 2-3 personal takeaways from this message?

_____

_____

_____

_____

_____

_____

_____

2. Did God speak to you in this message in any way? How so?

_____

_____

_____

_____

_____

_____

_____

3. How will these truths change the way you live?

_____

_____

_____

_____

_____

_____

YOUR STARTING PLACE: FULL SURRENDER TO JESUS

_____
_____
_____
_____
_____
_____
_____
_____
_____
_____
_____
_____
_____
_____
_____
_____
_____
_____
_____
_____
_____
_____

ENGAGING THE MESSAGE

1. What are your top 2-3 personal takeaways from this message?

_____

_____

_____

_____

_____

_____

2. Did God speak to you in this message in any way? How so?

_____

_____

_____

_____

_____

_____

3. How will these truths change the way you live?

_____

_____

_____

_____

_____

CORE TAKEAWAYS

- Full surrender to Jesus means He is King and Lord. It means He is the one in charge of our lives and leading our lives, not ourselves.

- Full surrender to Jesus is the launch pad for living the Christian life. If we have not fully surrendered our life to Jesus, we may find ourselves attempting to serve two masters. Jesus says that is not possible. He must be our first and highest love.

- Surrender to Jesus will (and should) change your life. You may find your priorities change, your values change, even your relationships. As we fully surrender our lives to Jesus as a living sacrifice, we should expect and be encouraged to see changes that reveal our deep love for Jesus.

Consider these common results of a fully surrendered life, and evaluate yourself. Have you experienced these in your life?

- Sensing inner peace

- Desiring to fight against your sin

- Experiencing God's love for you

- Desiring to engage the Bible

- Desiring to love others

- Making it a practice to obey the commands of Jesus

- Making intimacy with God a daily practice (reading the Bible, prayer, practicing God's presence everywhere)

- Living out the fruit of the Spirit: love, joy, peace, patience, kindness, goodness, faithfulness, gentleness, self-control

- Intentionally engaging in God's heart for the lost through sharing the good news of Jesus in word and serving to meet the needs of others in action

If you have not experienced these realities in your life, or your life has slipped away from them, you may need to fully surrender your life to Jesus. Consider praying this prayer:

Jesus, I give you my life, like a blank check. Everything I am, is yours. I surrender to you my whole life, my time, my talent, my wealth, my relationships, my plans, my future... everything. Everything is yours to use how you see fit.

OTHER HELPFUL RESOURCES

- *Four Chairs* by Adrian Despres (Forge)

- *Absolute Surrender* by Andrew Murray

- *Radical* by David Platt

- *No Compromise* by Melody Green

- *The Faith of Leap* by Michael Frost and Alan Hirsch

- *The Bravehearted Gospel* by Eric Ludy

KINGDOM LABORERSHIP

_____

_____

_____

_____

_____

_____

_____

_____

_____

_____

_____

_____

_____

_____

_____

_____

_____

_____

_____

_____

_____

_____

_____

_____

_____

_____

_____

_____

_____

_____

_____

_____

_____

ENGAGING THE MESSAGE

1. What are your top 2-3 personal takeaways from this message?

_____

_____

_____

_____

_____

_____

_____

2. Did God speak to you in this message in any way? How so?

_____

_____

_____

_____

_____

_____

_____

3. How will these truths change the way you live?

_____

_____

_____

_____

_____

_____

CORE TAKEAWAYS

- You are God's PLAN A for reaching the people around you, and there is no plan B.

- The prayer request for more laborers was Jesus' ONLY prayer request documented in the Bible.

- Note that Jesus say we needed more up-front, main-stage vocational church leaders. The word "laborer" is something anyone can become!... A Kingdom Laborer is an ordinary, everyday person who loves God, loves others, and advances the Kingdom wherever they go.

- Laborers utilize Jesus' method for loving those around them by seeing, stopping and spending time with people up-close, in the mainstream, one-life-at-a-time.

- Whatever their vocation or location, Laborers engage the "mudpuddles" of human need in front of them.

We may face common obstacles and excuses that hinder us from Kingdom Laborership, yet Jesus invites us into a life of purpose and Kingdom adventure when we get over ourselves:

- "I'm not perfect" – We point to Jesus, the only perfect one!

- "I'm not worthy" – We don't become Laborers because we are worthy, but because Jesus is worthy

- "My sin disqualifies me" – You have not lost your value to God

- "I don't know what to say" – Simply share your God-stories of how HE has shown up for you

- "Fear paralyzes me" – Ask God to help you, praying the *Ten-Finger prayer*, "I can do all things through Christ who strengthens me"

- "I don't feel qualified" – Jesus' method is simple... Get up close to people and let love tell you what to say or do.

Jesus' life reflects the high value of one-life-at-a-time ministry. Not everyone will stand in front of a large crowd, but everyone has a friend, neighbor, co-worker, family member, etc. who they can minister to.

OTHER HELPFUL RESOURCES

- *Plan A: Discovering Your Everyday, Everywhere Unique Ministry* by Dwight Robertson (Forge)

- *Mudrunner: Advancing the Kingdom No Matter the People, the Place, or the Cost* by Charlie Marq (Forge)

- *It's My Turn: 20 Kingdom Laborers Who Changed Their World and Compel Me to Impact Mine* by Forge

- *Multiplying Movements: A Discipleship Tool For Everyday Followers of Jesus* by Forge

ENGAGING THE WORD OF GOD

_____

_____

_____

_____

_____

_____

_____

_____

_____

_____

_____

_____

_____

_____

_____

_____

_____

_____

_____

_____

_____

ENGAGING THE MESSAGE

1. What are your top 2-3 personal takeaways from this message?

_____

_____

_____

_____

_____

_____

2. Did God speak to you in this message in any way? How so?

_____

_____

_____

_____

_____

_____

3. How will these truths change the way you live?

_____

_____

_____

_____

_____

CORE TAKEAWAYS

- The whole Bible is one unified story that leads to Jesus. Scripture is centered on Jesus – it all points to him (John 5:39-40).

- We study the Bible to: grow closer in relational intimacy with God (John 17:3), to build and strengthen our faith (Luke 6:46-49), and to be prepared for God's everyday mission (2 Timothy 3:16-17).

- God's word is intended to be put into action, not only read or listened to (James 1:22-25).

- The Bible should always be understood in context. Taking scripture out of context can lead to misinterpretation and misapplication of the text. We must understand a verse based on the verses and chapters around what we are reading.

- We should approach the word of God with humility, recognizing that we do not know everything and may have incorrect pre-suppositions, while the Bible itself is without error.

- Our lives should conform to God's word, whether we like or dislike something we read. It is crucial that we do not try to adapt God's word in order to make it more agreeable in our culture.

THE BIG PICTURE

You can understand the big picture of the Bible by breaking it into 4 parts:

1. **Creation**	Designed For Good Genesis 1-2
2. **The Fall**	Damaged By Evil Genesis 3, and Genesis 4—Malachi
3. **Redemption**	Redeemed for Good: Matthew—John and Sent to Heal: Acts—Revelation 20
4. **Restoration**	Revelation 21-22

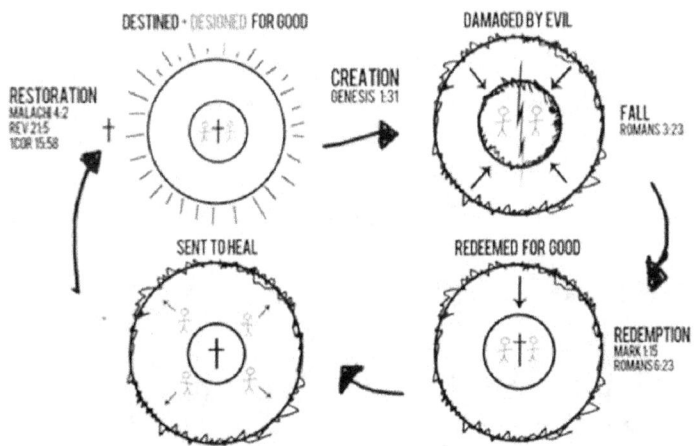

BIBLE STUDY METHODS

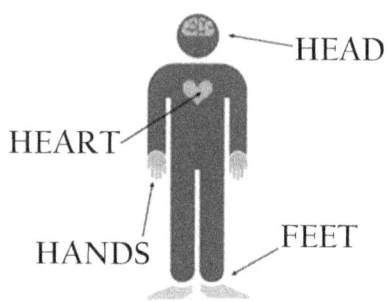

HEAD

What does the passage say?

What is the general message of the passage? Here are some helpful questions to ask to understand the message:

What is the context?

- Where does this passage fit into the big picture of the Bible?
- What happens before and after this passage?
- Where is it taking place?
- Who wrote it?
- Who was the original audience?

Who are the characters in the story?

- What do you observe about them?
- What did they do/say?
- What were they possibly feeling and thinking?
- What was the result of their words/actions?

What do we learn about God/Jesus/Holy Spirit in this passage?

What do we learn about humanity in this passage?

Do we learn anything about Satan or evil in this passage?

HEART

What Do I need to obey?

- What parts are jumping out to me?

- What is God speaking to me?

- In this passage: Is there a command to obey? A promise to hold onto/claim? An example to follow? Sin to confess?

- What needs to change in my life?

- Is there a character I most resonate or identity with?

HANDS

What practical action will I take?

- What will I do this week to apply and obey what God showed me?

FEET

Who can I share with?

- Who in my life do I need to share this message with?

BIBLE STUDY TIPS

- Choose a book and go through it. Don't simply rely on randomly opening to one verse here and there.

- Start with Mark, then read Acts, and then Ephesians. From there continue to read the remainder of the Bible until you finish it all. And then keep on reading, always!

- If you read 4 chapters per day, you will finish the entire Bible in less than 1 year. 3 Chapters OT and 1 chapter NT per day (book by book) OR simply choose one book at a time and read 4 chapters per day to finish in less than 1 year.

- Read for the plain meaning of the text.

- Get into the Word and get the Word into you!

OTHER HELPFUL RESOURCES

- *Blue Letter Bible* (BLB.org)—click Strong's using NASB version and you can lookup definitions from the original language.

- *Multiply* by Francis Chan—gives further book by book overview and Bible Study teaching.

- *How to Read the Bible for All Its Worth* by Gordon D. Fee and Douglas Stuart—further understanding how to engage the Bible. A free PDF: https://media.sabda.org/alkitab-2/PDF%20Books/00037%20Fee%20%26%20Stuart%20How%20to%20Read%20the%20Bible.pdf

- *Jesus On Every Page* by David Murray—discover how each part of the Bible points to Jesus.

- *Nave's Topical Bible*—helpful for studying topics throughout the entire Bible.

BRIEF SUMMARY FOR EACH BOOK IN THE BIBLE

Source: www.biblestudytools.com/books-of-the-bible

The Old Testament

(also known as the Jewish Tanakh) is the first 39 books in most Christian Bibles. The name stands for the original promise with God (to the descendants of Abraham in particular) prior to the coming of Jesus Christ in the New Testament (or the new promise). The Old Testament contains the creation of the universe, the history of the patriarchs, the exodus from Egypt, the formation of Israel as a nation, the subsequent decline and fall of the nation, the Prophets (who spoke for God), and the Wisdom Books:

Genesis
speaks of beginnings and is foundational to the understanding of the rest of the Bible. It is supremely a book that speaks about relationships, highlighting those between God and his creation, between God and humankind, and between human beings.

Exodus
describes the history of the Israelites leaving Egypt after slavery. The book lays a foundational theology in which God reveals his name, his attributes, his redemption, his law and how he is to be worshiped.

Leviticus
receives its name from the Septuagint (the pre-Christian Greek translation of the Old Testament) and means "concerning the Levites" (the priests of Israel). It serves as a manual of regulations enabling the holy King to set up his earthly throne among the people of his kingdom. It explains how they are to be his holy people and to worship him in a holy manner.

Numbers
relates the story of Israel's journey from Mount Sinai to the plains of Moab on the border of Canaan. The book tells of the murmuring and rebellion of God's people and of their subsequent judgment.

Deuteronomy
("repetition of the Law") serves as a reminder to God's people about His covenant. The book is a "pause" before Joshua's conquest begins and a reminder of what God required.

Joshua
is a story of conquest and fulfillment for the people of God. After many years of slavery in Egypt and 40 years in the desert, the Israelites were finally allowed to enter the land promised to their fathers.

Judges
depicts the life of Israel in the Promised Land—from the death of Joshua to the rise of the monarchy. It tells of urgent appeals to God in times of crisis and apostasy, moving the Lord to raise up leaders (judges) through whom He throws off foreign oppressors and restores the land to peace.

Ruth
has been called one of the best examples of short narrative ever written. It presents an account of the remnant of true faith and piety in the period of the judges through the fall and restoration of Naomi and her daughter-in-law Ruth (an ancestor of King David and Jesus).

1 Samuel
relates God's establishment of a political system in Israel headed by a human king. Through Samuel's life, we see the rise of the monarchy and the tragedy of its first king, Saul.

2 Samuel

depicts David as a true (though imperfect) representative of the ideal theocratic king, after the failure of King Saul. Under David's rule...

1 Kings

continues the account of the monarchy in Israel and God's involvement through the prophets. After David, his son Solomon ascends the throne of a united kingdom, but this unity only lasts during his reign. The book explores how each subsequent king in Israel and Judah answers God's call—or, as often happens, fails to listen. Lord caused the nation to prosper, to defeat its enemies, and to realize the fulfillment of His promises.

2 Kings

carries the historical account of Judah and Israel forward. The kings of each nation are judged in light of their obedience to the covenant with God. Ultimately, the people of both nations are exiled for disobedience.

1 Chronicles

was written as another history for the restored community, just as the author of Kings had organized and interpreted Israel's history to address the needs of the exiled community.

2 Chronicles

continues the account of Israel's history with an eye for restoration of those who had returned from exile.

Ezra

relates how God's covenant people were restored from Babylonian exile to the covenant land as a theocratic (kingdom of God) community even while continuing under foreign rule.

Nehemiah
being closely related to the book of Ezra, chronicles the return of this "cupbearer to the king" and the challenges he and the other Israelites face in their restored homeland.

Esther
records the institution of the annual festival of Purim through the historical account of Esther, a Jewish girl who becomes queen of Persia and saves her people from destruction.

Job
relates the account of a righteous man who suffers under terrible circumstances through a series of monologues. The book's profound insights, its literary structures, and the quality of its rhetoric display the author's genius.

Psalms
are collected songs and poems that represent centuries worth of praises and prayers to God on a number of themes and circumstances. The Psalms are impassioned, vivid and concrete; they are rich in images, in simile and metaphor.

Proverbs
was written to give "prudence to the simple, knowledge and discretion to the young," and to make the wise even wiser. The frequent references to "my son(s)" emphasize instructing the young and guiding them in a way of life that yields rewarding results.

Ecclesiastes
author puts his powers of wisdom to work to examine the human experience and assess the human situation. His perspective is limited to what happens "under the sun" (as is that of all human teachers).

Song of Solomon

In ancient Israel everything human came to expression in words: reverence, gratitude, anger, sorrow, suffering, trust, friendship, commitment. Here it is love that finds words–inspired words that disclose its exquisite charm and beauty as one of God's choicest gifts.

Isaiah

son of Amoz is often thought of as the greatest of the writing prophets. His name means "The Lord saves." Isaiah is a book that unveils the full dimensions of God's judgment and salvation.

Jeremiah

This book preserves an account of the prophetic ministry of Jeremiah, whose personal life and struggles are shown to us in greater depth and detail than those of any other Old Testament prophet.

Lamentations

consists of a series of poetic and powerful laments over the destruction of Jerusalem (the royal city of the Lord's kingdom) in 586 B.C.

Ezekiel

The Old Testament in general and the prophets in particular presuppose and teach God's sovereignty over all creation and the course of history. And nowhere in the Bible are God's initiative and control expressed more clearly and pervasively than in the book of the prophet Ezekiel.

Daniel

captures the major events in the life of the prophet Daniel during Israel's exile. His life and visions point to God's plans of redemption and sovereign control of history.

Hosea

The prophet Hosea son of Beeri lived in the tragic final days of the northern kingdom. His life served as a parable of God's faithfulness to an unfaithful Israel.

Joel

The prophet Joel warned the people of Judah about God's coming judgment—and the coming restoration and blessing that will come through repentance.

Amos

prophesied during the reigns of Uzziah over Judah (792-740 B.C.) and Jeroboam II over Israel (793-753).

Obadiah

The prophet Obadiah warned the proud people of Edom about the impending judgment coming upon them.

Jonah

is unusual as a prophetic book in that it is a narrative account of Jonah's mission to the city of Nineveh, his resistance, his imprisonment in a great fish, his visit to the city, and the subsequent outcome.

Micah

prophesied sometime between 750 and 686 B.C. during the reigns of Jotham, Ahaz, and Hezekiah, kings of Judah. Israel was in an apostate condition. Micah predicted the fall of her capital, Samaria, and also foretold the inevitable desolation of Judah.

Nahum

The book contains the "vision of Nahum," whose name means "comfort." The focal point of the entire book is the Lord's judgment on Nineveh for her oppression, cruelty, idolatry, and wickedness.

Habakkuk

Little is known about Habakkuk except that he was a contemporary of Jeremiah and a man of vigorous faith. The book bearing his name contains a dialogue between the prophet and God concerning injustice and suffering.

Zephaniah

The prophet Zephaniah was evidently a person of considerable social standing in Judah and was probably related to the royal line. The intent of the author was to announce to Judah God's approaching judgment.

Haggai

was a prophet who, along with Zechariah, encouraged the returned exiles to rebuild the temple. His prophecies clearly show the consequences of disobedience. When the people give priority to God and his house, they are blessed.

Zechariah

Like Jeremiah and Ezekiel, Zechariah was not only a prophet, but also a member of a priestly family. The chief purpose of Zechariah (and Haggai) was to rebuke the people of Judah and to encourage and motivate them to complete the rebuilding of the temple.

Malachi

whose name means "my messenger," spoke to the Israelites after their return from exile. The theological message of the book can be summed up in one sentence: The Great King will come not only to judge his people, but also to bless and restore them.

The New Testament

is a collection of 27 books, usually placed after the Old
Testament in most Christian Bibles. The name refers to the new
covenant (or promise) between God and humanity through the
death and resurrection of Jesus Christ. The New Testament
chronicles the life and ministry of Jesus, the growth and impact
of the early church, and instructive letters to early churches:

Matthew

Matthew's main purpose in writing his Gospel (the "good news") is to
prove to his Jewish readers that Jesus is their Messiah. He does this
primarily by showing how Jesus in his life and ministry fulfilled the
Old Testament Scriptures.

Mark

Since Mark's Gospel (the "good news") is traditionally associated with
Rome, it may have been occasioned by the persecutions of the Roman
church in the period c. A.D. 64-67. Mark may be writing to prepare his
readers for such suffering by placing before them the life of our Lord.

Luke

Luke's Gospel (the "good news") was written to strengthen the faith of
all believers and to answer the attacks of unbelievers. It was presented
to debunk some disconnected and ill-founded reports about Jesus.
Luke wanted to show that the place of the Gentile (non-Jewish)
Christian in God's kingdom is based on the teaching of Jesus.

John

John's Gospel (the "good news") is rather different from the other three,
highlighting events not detailed in the others. The author himself
states his main purpose clearly in 20:31: "that you may believe that Jesus
is the Christ, the Son of God, and that by believing you may have life in
his name."

Acts

The book of Acts provides a bridge for the writings of the New Testament. As a second volume to Luke's Gospel, it joins what Jesus "began to do and to teach" as told in the Gospels with what he continued to do and teach through the apostles' preaching and the establishment of the church.

Romans

Paul's primary theme in Romans is presenting the gospel (the "good news"), God's plan of salvation and righteousness for all humankind, Jew and non-Jew alike.

1 Corinthians

The first letter to the Corinthians revolves around the theme of problems in Christian conduct in the church. It thus has to do with progressive sanctification, the continuing development of a holy character. Obviously Paul was personally concerned with the Corinthians' problems, revealing a true pastor's (shepherd's) heart.

2 Corinthians

Because of the occasion that prompted this letter, Paul had a number of purposes in mind: to express the comfort and joy Paul felt because the Corinthians had responded favorably to his painful letter; to let them know about the trouble he went through in the province of Asia; and to explain to them the true nature (its joys, sufferings and rewards) and high calling of Christian ministry.

Galatians

stands as an eloquent and vigorous apologetic for the essential New Testament truth that people are justified by faith in Jesus Christ—by nothing less and nothing more—and that they are sanctified not by legalistic works but by the obedience that comes from faith in God's work for them.

Ephesians

Unlike several of the other letters Paul wrote, Ephesians does not address any particular error or heresy. Paul wrote to expand the horizons of his readers, so that they might understand better the dimensions of God's eternal purpose and grace and come to appreciate the high goals God has for the church.

Philippians

Paul's primary purpose in writing this letter was to thank the Philippians for the gift they had sent him upon learning of his detention at Rome. However, he makes use of this occasion to fulfill several other desires: (1) to report on his own circumstances; (2) to encourage the Philippians to stand firm in the face of persecution and rejoice regardless of circumstances; and (3) to exhort them to humility and unity.

Colossians

Paul's purpose is to refute the Colossian heresy. To accomplish this goal, he exalts Christ as the very image of God, the Creator, the preexistent sustainer of all things, the head of the church, the first to be resurrected, the fullness of deity (God) in bodily form, and the reconciler.

1 Thessalonians

Although the thrust of the letter is varied, the subject of eschatology (doctrine of last things) seems to be predominant in both Thessalonian letters. Every chapter of 1 Thessalonians ends with a reference to the second coming of Christ.

2 Thessalonians

Since the situation in the Thessalonian church has not changed substantially, Paul's purpose in writing is very much the same as in his first letter to them. He writes (1) to encourage persecuted believers, (2) to correct a misunderstanding concerning the Lord's return, and (3) to exhort the Thessalonians to be steadfast and to work for a living.

1 Timothy

During his fourth missionary journey, Paul had instructed Timothy to care for the church at Ephesus while he went on to Macedonia. When he realized that he might not return to Ephesus in the near future, he wrote this first letter to Timothy to develop the charge he had given his young assistant. This is the first of the "Pastoral Epistles."

2 Timothy

Paul was concerned about the welfare of the churches during this time of persecution under Nero, and he admonishes Timothy to guard the gospel, to persevere in it, to keep on preaching it, and, if necessary, to suffer for it. This is the second "Pastoral Epistle."

Titus

Apparently Paul introduced Christianity in Crete when he and Titus visited the island, after which he left Titus there to organize the converts. Paul sent the letter with Zenas and Apollos, who were on a journey that took them through Crete, to give Titus personal authorization and guidance in meeting opposition, instructions about faith and conduct, and warnings about false teachers. This is the last of the "Pastoral Epistles."

Philemon

To win Philemon's willing acceptance of the runaway slave Onesimus, Paul writes very tactfully and in a lighthearted tone, which he creates with wordplay. The appeal is organized in a way prescribed by ancient Greek and Roman teachers: to build rapport, to persuade the mind, and to move the emotions.

Hebrews

The theme of Hebrews is the absolute supremacy and sufficiency of Jesus Christ as revealer and as mediator of God's grace. A striking feature of this presentation of the gospel is the unique manner in which the author employs expositions of eight specific passages of the Old Testament Scriptures.

James

Characteristics that make the letter distinctive are: (1) its unmistakably Jewish nature; (2) its emphasis on vital Christianity, characterized by good deeds and a faith that works (genuine faith must and will be accompanied by a consistent lifestyle); (3) its simple organization; (4) and its familiarity with Jesus' teachings preserved in the Sermon on the Mount.

1 Peter

Although 1 Peter is a short letter, it touches on various doctrines and has much to say about Christian life and duties. It is not surprising that different readers have found it to have different principal themes. For example, it has been characterized as a letter of separation, of suffering and persecution, of suffering and glory, of hope, of pilgrimage, of courage, and as a letter dealing with the true grace of God.

2 Peter

In his first letter Peter feeds Christ's sheep by instructing them how to deal with persecution from outside the church; in this second letter he teaches them how to deal with false teachers and evildoers who have come into the church.

1 John

John's readers were confronted with an early form of Gnostic teaching of the Corinthian variety. This heresy was also libertine, throwing off all moral restraints. Consequently, John wrote this letter with two basic purposes in mind: (1) to expose false teachers and (2) to give believers assurance of salvation.

2 John

During the first two centuries the gospel was taken from place to place by traveling evangelists and teachers. Believers customarily took these missionaries into their homes and gave them provisions for their journey when they left. Since Gnostic teachers also relied on this practice, 2 John was written to urge discernment in supporting traveling teachers.

3 John

Itinerant teachers sent out by John were rejected in one of the churches in the province of Asia by a dictatorial leader, Diotrephes, who even excommunicated members who showed hospitality to John's messengers. John wrote this letter to commend Gaius for supporting the teachers and, indirectly, to warn Diotrephes.

Jude

Although Jude was very eager to write to his readers about salvation, he felt that he must instead warn them about certain immoral men circulating among them who were perverting the grace of God. Apparently these false teachers were trying to convince believers that being saved by grace gave them license to sin since their sins would no longer be held against them.

Revelation

John writes to encourage the faithful to resist staunchly the demands of emperor worship. He informs his readers that the final showdown between God and Satan is imminent. Satan will increase his persecution of believers, but they must stand fast, even to death. They are sealed against any spiritual harm and will soon be vindicated when Christ returns, when the wicked are forever destroyed, and when God's people enter an eternity of glory and blessedness.

GOD'S VOICE

_____
_____
_____
_____
_____
_____
_____
_____
_____
_____
_____
_____
_____
_____
_____
_____
_____
_____
_____
_____

ENGAGING THE MESSAGE

1. What are your top 2-3 personal takeaways from this message?

_____

_____

_____

_____

_____

_____

_____

2. Did God speak to you in this message in any way? How so?

_____

_____

_____

_____

_____

_____

_____

3. How will these truths change the way you live?

_____

_____

_____

_____

_____

_____

CORE TAKEAWAYS

4 Common Ways God Speaks to Us:

The Bible: God always communicates to us through the plain meaning of Scripture and also through Scripture penetrating our hearts based on our specific circumstances. (2 Timothy 3:16; Psalm 19:10-12)

Whispers: The still small voice of God often comes through a gentle nudge inside, something going off in your spirit like a soft beeping alarm, or thoughts that are not our own but from the Holy Spirit, or a gentle nudge inside. (Mark 13:11; Acts 8:29; Acts 13:2; Acts 20:23)

Images: Dreams as we sleep or visions that we see while awake, almost as if they are in our imagination, can be from God. (Acts 16:9-10; Acts 2:17; Acts 10:9-18)

Burdens: You may feel overwhelming compassion, heavyhearted, or compelled by God that you must do something. (Acts 20:22; Jeremiah 20:9; Matthew 9:36; Luke 19:41-46)

Is it Really God? — A Quick Test:
1. Does it line up with the teachings of the Bible?
2. Does it glorify God?
3. Does it advance His Kingdom (rather than my own agenda)?

Ask God often, "Do you have anything to speak to me?" If nothing comes to mind, simply make the wisest choices you can.

LISTENING TO GOD EXERCISE

- **Grab a journal.** Pray, asking the Lord in Jesus' name to silence your flesh and the enemy. Ask God to speak to you, and ask that you hear His voice alone. Maybe you have a specific question, or maybe you just want to ask if God has anything to say to you.

- **Listen.** Write down whatever comes to mind. Make sure it is truly God speaking by confirming what you heard aligns with the teaching of the Bible, that it comes with the peace of Christ, and that it glorifies God not yourself.

- **Receive whatever you hear God saying.** And when applicable, commit to obey it. Make this a regular practice in your life!

OTHER HELPFUL RESOURCES

- *Let God Guide You Daily* by Wesley Duewel

- *Is That Really You, God?* by Loren Cunningham

- *Listening to God* by Charles Stanley

INTIMACY WITH GOD

_____

_____

_____

_____

_____

_____

_____

_____

_____

_____

_____

_____

_____

_____

_____

_____

_____

_____

_____

_____

ENGAGING THE MESSAGE

1. What are your top 2-3 personal takeaways from this message?

_____

_____

_____

_____

_____

_____

_____

2. Did God speak to you in this message in any way? How so?

_____

_____

_____

_____

_____

_____

_____

3. How will these truths change the way you live?

_____

_____

_____

_____

_____

_____

CORE TAKEAWAYS

- The greatest gift you will ever give the world is your intimacy with God!

- Intimacy with God is a daily practice, both for time alone with God and practicing His presence along the way, wherever we go!

- We also need to create space for *extended* time alone with God, just as Jesus often slipped away to pray (Luke 5:16). Making this time a priority is essential to the Christian walk.

- Schedule in extended times alone with God on your calendar on a regular basis (such as every quarter). We call them Dates Alone with God or D.A.W.G.s.

- Potential Packing List for a Date Alone With God (This list isn't definitive—it's just a quick reference to jog your memory or help you brainstorm some things you might want to take when you're ready to prepare for your own date with God!)

— Packing List —

- Bible
- Journal and pen
- Prayer list
- Notecards for writing encouragement notes
- Spiritual-growth book or magazine
- Music / Worship playlist
- Musical instrument / Hymnal or book of praise songs
- Blanket or chair for outdoor locations

- Weather-appropriate gear for outdoor locations (sweatshirt, sunglasses, sunblock, etc.)
- Snacks

Practical ways to seek intimacy with God include: prayer, Scripture, musical worship, obedience to Jesus, silence focused on God, listening for His promptings, and more. YET, the goal of our love must always be seeking Jesus Himself.

Intimacy with God is the bedrock upon which your entire life and ministry will be built. Without intimacy it will be impossible to accomplish what God is calling you to.

OTHER HELPFUL RESOURCES

- *Practicing God's Presence* by Robert Elmer on the life of Brother Lawrence

- *Is God Waiting For a Date With You?* by Dwight Robertson (Forge)

- *Forged by Fire: Making Intimacy with God Your Greatest Gift* by Dwight Robertson (Forge)

- *Spiritual Life Notebook* by Forge

- *Hudson Taylors Spiritual Secret* by Dr. & Mrs. Taylor

- *Discipled by Jesus* by Robert Gelinas

OVERCOMING HINDERANCES

_____

_____

_____

_____

_____

_____

_____

_____

_____

_____

_____

_____

_____

_____

_____

_____

_____

_____

_____

_____

_____

_____

_____

ENGAGING THE MESSAGE

1. What are your top 2-3 personal takeaways from this message?

_____
_____
_____
_____
_____
_____
_____

2. Did God speak to you in this message in any way? How so?

_____
_____
_____
_____
_____
_____
_____

3. How will these truths change the way you live?

_____
_____
_____
_____
_____
_____

CORE TAKEAWAYS

- We must throw off everything that hinders us, so that we can run in God's purpose for our lives! (Hebrews 12:1)

- We can only throw off everything that hinders by looking to Jesus (Hebrews 12:2-3)

Main hindrances and what we should do with them:

- **Unconfessed Sin** (1 John 1:8-9; James 5:16)... Confess our sin: "Lord I'm sorry for..."

- **Believing Lies** (John 8:32)... Rebuke lies and receive God's truth: "Lord, in Jesus' name I rebuke the lie that... and trust in your truth that..."

- **Unforgiveness** (Colossians 3:13)... Forgive those who have wronged you: "Lord, I forgive [person's name] for hurting me in this way..."

- **Generational Patterns** (1 Peter 1:18)... Rebuke negative generational patterns and embrace God's plans and blessings for your future: "Lord, in Jesus' name, I rebuke the family pattern of... that has been passed to me, and ask that in place of that your blessings and Kingdom pattern would pass through my life in the future."

- **Ungodly Relationships** (1 Corinthians 15:33; 1 Corinthians 6:16; Ephesians 5:22-28, 6:1-4; 1 Peter 3:7)... Leave behind ungodly relationships and seek out Godly ones: "Lord, help me to break off ungodly relationships that are hindering my life. Would you restore back to my heart what should not have been given away?"

- **Attacks of the Enemy** (1 Peter 5:8; Ephesians 4:26; James 4:7)... Rebuke the enemy's attack in your life and walk in the Spirit: "In Jesus' name go away! I rebuke any attack of the enemy in my life. Lord, would you fill me with your Spirit and protect me with your armor?"

Spend time praying and ask Jesus, "What are the hindrances in my life right now?" In prayer, Biblically deal with each one that comes to mind (as outlined above).

Dealing with these types of hindrances is not a one and done event. We must continue to throw off everything that hinders, fixing our eyes on Jesus, and doing what He has asked us to do for His Kingdom advancement! When spiritual hindrances arise, deal with them immediately in prayer.

PRAYER

_____

_____

_____

_____

_____

_____

_____

_____

_____

_____

_____

_____

_____

_____

_____

_____

_____

_____

ENGAGING THE MESSAGE

1. What are your top 2-3 personal takeaways from this message?

_____

_____

_____

_____

_____

_____

_____

2. Did God speak to you in this message in any way? How so?

_____

_____

_____

_____

_____

_____

_____

3. How will these truths change the way you live?

_____

_____

_____

_____

_____

_____

CORE TAKEWAYS

- Prayer is a lifestyle and a conversation with God

- We must pray with perseverance ("seek, ask knock"), in His name (His character / will), and in the Spirit (by His leading)... Don't just see the problems; pray the solutions!

- Pray specifically (not only vaguely and generally, i.e., "God bless..."), so that you know how God answers your prayers, building your faith and giving God glory!

- Prayer is a two-way conversation with God. We speak and share but also listen for what He has to say.

- Pray in your normal language. God isn't looking for special, professional, or fancy language, but an open worshipful heart. Freely share your heart and mind with God.

Check out Matthew 6:9-13 and consider using the acronym P.R.A.Y. to guide your prayer times:

- **Praise** – Reminding ourselves of who God is as we tell Him who He is, lifting our eyes to Him!

- **Repent** – We must confess our sins and forgive those who have wronged us, receiving His light and cleansing in our hearts

- **Ask** – Seek God for your daily needs and requests

- **Yield** – "not my will but yours be done." Sometimes God will say "no" to our requests because He knows what is best and has a plan we do not always know

OTHER HELPFUL RESOURCES

- *Ten-Finger Prayers: The Amazingly True Story of How An Orphan Became An Overcomer* by Agnes Robertson (Forge)

- *With Christ in the School of Prayer* by Andrew Murray

- *Why Revival Tarries* by Leonard Ravenhill

- *Touch The World Through Prayer* by Wesley Duewel

- *Mighty Prevailing Prayer* by Wesley Duewel

- *Fresh Wind, Fresh Fire* by Jim Cymbala

- *Victorious Praying* by Bill Thrasher

- *Wrestling Prayer* by Eric and Leslie Ludy

- E.M. Bounds on Prayer

PRAISE

_____

_____

_____

_____

_____

_____

_____

_____

_____

_____

_____

_____

_____

_____

_____

_____

_____

_____

_____

_____

_____

ENGAGING THE MESSAGE

1. What are your top 2-3 personal takeaways from this message?

_____
_____
_____
_____
_____
_____
_____

2. Did God speak to you in this message in any way? How so?

_____
_____
_____
_____
_____
_____
_____

3. How will these truths change the way you live?

_____
_____
_____
_____
_____
_____

CORE TAKEAWAYS

- Praise is a decision that sets our eyes on God, trusting who He is. Praise helps us take our eyes off difficult situations and put them on the one who brings us hope in the midst of difficulty.

- Praise results in enjoyment of God. When God 'demands' praise he is inviting us to enjoy him:

C.S. Lewis, in his book Reflections On The Psalms, says he had a hard time with the thought that we are supposed to praise God, especially the notion that God demanded it. He knew that God didn't need our praise, but he didn't understand why He asked for it:

> The most obvious fact about praise—whether about God or anything else— had strangely escaped me. I thought of it in terms of a compliment, approval, or the giving of honor. I had never noticed that all enjoyment spontaneously overflows into praise. The world rings with praise ... lovers praising their mistresses the ones they love, readers praising their favorite poet, walkers praising the countryside, players praising their favorite game. I had not noticed how the humblest, and at the same time most balanced and capacious minds, praised least. I had not noticed, either, that just as men spontaneously praise whatever they value, so they spontaneously urge us to join them in praising it: "Isn't she lovely? Wasn't it glorious? Don't you think that magnificent?" The Psalmists, in telling everyone to praise God, are doing what all men do when they speak of what they care about. I think we delight to praise what we enjoy because the praise not merely expresses, but completes the enjoyment. It's not out of compliment that lovers keep on telling one another how beautiful they are; their delight is incomplete till it is expressed! To fully enjoy is to communicate our love. In commanding us to communicate our love for Him, God is inviting us to enjoy Him.

- Praise renews our spiritual strength (Psalm 149:6 and Isaiah 40:29-31, Nehemiah 8:10) Reviving, refreshing, and empowering us to fully engage God and his mission.

- Praise clarifies your vision and sets our eyes above (Colossians 3:2), moving your thoughts toward *whose* you are, off your flesh and onto His power!

- Praise empowers your prayer life! "When I cannot pray I always sing – it brings heavens power upon me" – Martin Luther

- Praise is a weapon in spiritual warfare, repelling the darkness of Satan and his demons. In moments of increased spiritual attack, praise brings peace and rest.

- Praise Connects us with the presence of God (Psalm 22:3)

SUGGESTIONS FOR PERSONAL PRAISE TIMES

- Read a Hymn.

- Use memorized Scriptures to praise God.

- Make a thanksgiving "Miracle List"... (answers to prayer and monumental spiritual milestones God brought about).

- Use "The Alphabet": "Lord, you are 'A' for "A_____,"
  "Lord, you 'B' for "B_____.""

- Surround your life with praise music.

- Treat it like a financial "Bill Due"—"Give God the glory DUE His Name."

PASSION

_____
_____
_____
_____
_____
_____
_____
_____
_____
_____
_____
_____
_____
_____
_____
_____
_____
_____
_____
_____
_____

ENGAGING THE MESSAGE

1. What are your top 2-3 personal takeaways from this message?

_____

_____

_____

_____

_____

_____

_____

2. Did God speak to you in this message in any way? How so?

_____

_____

_____

_____

_____

_____

_____

3. How will these truths change the way you live?

_____

_____

_____

_____

_____

CORE TAKEAWAYS

- "Passion" is the amount of suffering you would delight in to achieve a goal (2 Corinthians 12:10)... Do I truly experience joy when I suffer?

- True passion makes suffering look like entertainment... am I truly passionate for Christ?

- Suffering is a gift of God to us, alongside salvation (Philippians 1:29)

- Are you willing to say to God: I will engage ANYONE, go ANYWHERE, do ANYTHING, at ANYTIME... for you and your Kingdom cause!

- Until I can say "whatever," "wherever," "whenever," "however"; I have not graduated into "university love" for God.

- Take note of Jesus' words in Luke 9:57–62. Many thought they would follow, but when Jesus told them the cost they did not follow. Yet those who embraced the call of Jesus, no matter the cost, experienced a life full of joy, purpose, and the greatest Kingdom adventure they could ever imagine!

OTHER HELPFUL RESOURCES

- *The Normal Christian Life* by Watchman Nee

- *The Cost of Discipleship* by Dietrich Bonhoeffer

SHARING MY GOD-STORY

Our God-stories are one of the best ways to reach the lost and bridge them to the gospel message ...

- A God-story can be a moment you first believed, a moment where you 'went all in'/surrendered to Jesus, or simply a time when God really showed up for you!

- Your God story (or God stories) should highlight the CHANGE that happened in your life as a result of encountering or surrendering to Jesus.

- Keep it short—people are busy, and tend to only be able to hear what you have to say if it is short. You can always share more later as people are interested.

- We can share anywhere, anytime, with anyone. We can share our Jesus-stories in just a short couple minutes.

The *3 Elements* you should include in your story:

1 | How would you characterize yourself before encountering Jesus? (For Example: fear-filled, prideful, depressed, angry, etc.)

2 | How did you encounter Jesus? (For Example: Prayer, a sermon, a friend, etc.)

3 | How did you and your life change as a result of encountering Jesus? (For Example: fear to courage, depression to joy, anger to forgiveness, anxiety to peace, pride to humility)

- After you share your story, share the simple gospel message in this practical way: "This was possible in my life because Jesus died on the cross for our sins, which separated us from the one true God. Jesus then rose from the dead, so He is alive today and waiting for relationship with us. He loves us! And do not forget to end with a question: "Is this something you are interested in? Do you want Jesus to change your life too?"

After you share your story and asking them if they want to also follow Jesus, they may have various responses:

- **"I am ready to follow Jesus."** — Pray together with them right then! Say something like this to encourage them to begin a relationship with Jesus, "Why don't you pray out loud with me right now and tell Jesus something like this in your own words: 'Jesus, I believe you died on the cross for my sin and rose from the dead. Today I want to begin a relationship with you. I submit my life to follow you.'" (This concept comes from Romans 10:9). (Once someone believes in Jesus, begin going through this *Multiplying Movements* tool with them starting at Episode I so that they too can become a laborer for God's Kingdom!)

- **"I do not want to follow Jesus. I am not interested."** – If someone is not ready to follow Jesus and not interested in learning more, then simply continue to love them in action, continue to share different stories of Jesus at work in your life as you get the chance, and most importantly keep praying!

- **"I'm not ready to follow Jesus yet, but I'm interested in learning more."** – You might find someone fumbling a little bit between being ready to follow Jesus and unsure if they are ready. If this is the case, you can ask a simple question like "What is holding you back from following Jesus?" and then discuss whatever that is. It could be that this simple conversation removes their obstacle to following Jesus and they decide to believe! In other cases, they might need more time before deciding to follow Jesus. If this is the case, ask them to begin meeting with you regularly to explore what Jesus is all about and discuss any questions they may have. (See Episode II "Reaching the Lost" of "Multiplying Movements" by Forge for tips on how to meet with this person, and a list of Bible stories you can use to discuss with this interested person.

WRITING OUT MY GOD STORY

- Write out each part of your God-story in the three sections below.

My story *before* **encountering Jesus:**

_____
_____
_____
_____
_____
_____
_____
_____
_____
_____

How I encountered Jesus:

_____
_____
_____
_____
_____
_____
_____
_____
_____
_____

How my life has changed *after* encountering Jesus:

_____
_____
_____
_____
_____
_____
_____
_____
_____
_____
_____
_____

My God-Story: putting it all together

- On the next page, combine the 3 parts to make 1 unified story.

MY GOD STORY

_____
_____
_____
_____
_____
_____
_____
_____
_____
_____
_____
_____
_____
_____
_____
_____
_____
_____
_____
_____
_____
_____
_____
_____
_____
_____
_____
_____
_____
_____

ENGAGING THE MESSAGE

1. What are your top 2-3 personal takeaways from this message?

_____
_____
_____
_____
_____
_____
_____

2. Did God speak to you in this message in any way? How so?

_____
_____
_____
_____
_____
_____
_____

3. How will these truths change the way you live?

_____
_____
_____
_____
_____
_____

FAITH OVER FEAR

ENGAGING THE MESSAGE

1. What are your top 2-3 personal takeaways from this message?

_____

_____

_____

_____

_____

_____

_____

2. Did God speak to you in this message in any way? How so?

_____

_____

_____

_____

_____

_____

_____

3. How will these truths change the way you live?

_____

_____

_____

_____

_____

_____

CORE TAKEAWAYS

- Fear is a common human experience. Often fear compels us to go nowhere, be nobody, and do nothing. It is paralyzing.

- As followers of Jesus, it is crucial for us to choose faith in Jesus over fear of our circumstances. Though fear is powerful, Jesus is more powerful.

- With Jesus, we can walk forward in courage, knowing that He is with us. He will never leave us nor forsake us. We don't have to trust in who we are, because we can trust in who God is (Psalm 121)

- God has not given us a spirit of fear... (2 Timothy 1:7)

- Perfect love casts out all fear... (1 John 4:18)

THE GOSPEL

_____

_____

_____

_____

_____

_____

_____

_____

_____

_____

_____

_____

_____

_____

_____

_____

_____

_____

_____

ENGAGING THE MESSAGE

1. What are your top 2-3 personal takeaways from this message?

_____

_____

_____

_____

_____

_____

_____

2. Did God speak to you in this message in any way? How so?

_____

_____

_____

_____

_____

_____

_____

3. How will these truths change the way you live?

_____

_____

_____

_____

_____

_____

CORE TAKEAWAYS

- The word we translate as "gospel" literally means "good news." In the Greek speaking world of the New Testament, this word was used in the context of Kings, especially in to announce a new king or a military victory. In the New Testament this is also true. The word "gospel" is used so that we understand that Jesus is a King victoriously establishing His Kingdom.

The simple gospel is the message that Jesus died, was buried, and three days later rose again, proving that He really is King and Lord of all! (1 Corinthians 15:1-4; Mark 1:14-15)

- **Died** – Jesus was crucified by the Romans. This was an excruciating torturous death. No one could survive this.

- **Buried** – Jesus was actually dead. He did not fake his death, He was not almost dead, nor just severely injured. Jesus was truly dead.

- **Rose again** – This is the most important element of the gospel. If Jesus didn't actually rise from the dead, then he was not really God, which means His message was false, and He was either a liar or lunatic. This also means that Christians would be following a false god, and not really saved from sin. BUT, because Jesus did rise from the dead, we can be confident that Jesus really is who He says he is, that he really did pay the price for our sins and we really are following the one true God.

This good news of Jesus as King should impact every aspect of our life.

- It should impact our relationships: parents, spouse, believers, unbelievers, everyone!

- It should impact how we spend our lives; our time, our money, our energy.

- Ultimately the good news should impact everything about us and drive us to Love God, Love others, and advance the Kingdom every day, everywhere

OTHER HELPFUL RESOURCES

- *The Case for the Resurrection of Jesus* by Gary Habermas & Michael Licona

- *Verdict of History* by Gary Habermas

- *The Resurrection of Jesus* by Michael Licona

- *Case for Christ* by Lee Strobel

- www.DesiringGod.org/messages/is-the-kingdom-present-or-future

- James Choung: The Big Story YouTube videos

- James Choung content/books: www.jameschoung.net

- TonyEvans.org/the-kingdom-has-come

HUMILITY

_____

_____

_____

_____

_____

_____

_____

_____

_____

_____

_____

_____

_____

_____

_____

_____

_____

_____

_____

_____

_____

ENGAGING THE MESSAGE

1. What are your top 2-3 personal takeaways from this message?

_____

_____

_____

_____

_____

_____

_____

2. Did God speak to you in this message in any way? How so?

_____

_____

_____

_____

_____

_____

_____

3. How will these truths change the way you live?

_____

_____

_____

_____

_____

_____

CORE TAKEAWAYS

- **Definition of Humility:** Not thinking less of yourself, but thinking of yourself less.

- Humility is focused on Jesus and others before self.

- Jesus is the best example of humility. He, the God of the universe, stepped fully into human life. Humility is not merely about service or outward appearances. True humility starts in the heart and mind. A truly humble person considers others more significant than themselves. (Philippians 2:3-8)

- Humility is at the heart of Laborership. Humble laborers are not focused on lifting themselves up but of making much of Jesus, as they serve, love, and seek to empower others. (Matthew 20:25-28; Matthew 23:8-12; Colossians 3:12)

OTHER HELPFUL RESOURCES

- "Humility" Sermon by Olivia Humphrey (on the Forge YouTube Channel: YouTube.com/ForgeForward)

- *Humility: The Beauty of Holiness* by Andrew Murray

- *Humility: True Greatness* by CJ Mahaney

GOD'S HEART FOR ALL NATIONS

_____

_____

_____

_____

_____

_____

_____

_____

_____

_____

_____

_____

_____

_____

_____

_____

_____

_____

_____

_____

ENGAGING THE MESSAGE

1. What are your top 2-3 personal takeaways from this message?

_____

_____

_____

_____

_____

_____

_____

2. Did God speak to you in this message in any way? How so?

_____

_____

_____

_____

_____

_____

_____

3. How will these truths change the way you live?

_____

_____

_____

_____

_____

_____

CORE TAKEAWAYS

- Throughout the Scriptures, God has always had a heart for all nations. The Biblical word "nations" does not mean geo-political nations as we understand them today, but rather means "ethno-linguistic people groups," which are groups of people with the same language, culture, and ethnicity. You might be able to call these "tribes."

- From the book of Genesis all the way to Revelation we see God's heart for all people, everywhere!

- All throughout the Scriptures, God calls on his followers to reveal Him to the world. God wants us to take on his burden for all people, everywhere to know him.

As followers of Jesus there are at least 3 ways we can respond to God's heart for all people:

- **Go** – We personally carry the message of Jesus to people groups who do not yet have it.

- **Send** – We can encourage, financially support, pray for, equip / mobilize others to go, and creatively partner (opening a business branch / letting someone going use your business name or connection, invent creative mission resources or technology, use technological skills to get the message into restricted places and systems, spread the word through photo and video to support the mission, etc.)

- **Disobey** — all followers of Jesus are commissioned to either, go, send, or do some mixture of the two. If we don't engage in one or the other of these calls, we are disobeying.

We can become exposed to God's heart for all nations and for the unreached by:

- taking a short-term mission trip, researching mission organizations
- researching other religions and evangelism/apologetics methods for engaging them
- finding refugees and immigrants from unreached nations in a city near my home
- exploring the interactive maps on JoshuaProject.net or PeopleGroups.org, and more...

- No matter what is going on in the world, our role is to get the message of Jesus to every people group on the planet (Matthew 24:14)!

- "The great commission is not an option to be considered but a command to be obeyed" – Hudson Taylor on Matthew 28:19

OTHER HELPFUL RESOURCES

- *Mudrunner: Advancing the Kingdom No Matter the People, the Place, or the Cost* by Charlie Marq (Forge)

- How to Send: *Gospel Patrons* by John Rinehart

- People Group Statistics: www.JoshuaProject.net or PeopleGroups.org

- World Prayer Book: *Operation World* by Jason Madryk

- *Perspectives: On The World Christian Movement* by Ralph Winter and Steven C. Hawthorne

- *Dangerous* by Caleb Bislow

- *Eternity in Their Hearts* by Don Richardson

- *Let the Nations Be Glad* by John Piper

- *The Insanity of God* by Nik Ripken

- *Miraculous Movements* by Jerry Trousdale

SPIRITUAL WARFARE

_____

_____

_____

_____

_____

_____

_____

_____

_____

_____

_____

_____

_____

_____

_____

_____

_____

_____

_____

_____

_____

_____

_____

_____

ENGAGING THE MESSAGE

1. What are your top 2-3 personal takeaways from this message?

_____

_____

_____

_____

_____

_____

_____

2. Did God speak to you in this message in any way? How so?

_____

_____

_____

_____

_____

_____

_____

3. How will these truths change the way you live?

_____

_____

_____

_____

_____

_____

CORE TAKEWAYS

- Spiritual warfare is real (1 Peter 5:8-10)

- Satan desires to steal kill and destroy. He is a liar, murderer, and accuser. (John 10:10; John 8:44; Revelation 12:10)

- Jesus is victorious and all powerful, so we don't need to fear (Revelation 19:11–16; 2 Timothy 1:7)

- Through Christ we can have victory in the midst of this warfare

- While you cannot be "possessed" (meaning ownership) by the enemy when you are a believer, Satan desires to influence you by creating strongholds and footholds in your life (Ephesians 4:26-27)

- Satan will also seek to create obstacles and attacks in your life as you advance God's Kingdom (Revelation 12:17), so that he can keep unbelievers blinded from the gospel (2 Corinthians 4:4-5)

- We must submit to God and resist the devil... when attacked, say out loud "Jesus help me. In Jesus' name I command any spirit to leave!" (James 4:6).

WEAPONS OF OUR WARFARE

- **The Word of God**: Jesus fought the enemy using memorized Scripture (Matthew 4:1-11). Quote the truth of God's Word out loud!

- **The Name of Jesus**. His name and authority was used out loud by His followers in the Gospels and Acts (Acts 16:18). Speak the name of Jesus out loud. We have authority over spiritual forces as followers of Jesus. If we speak in the name of Jesus the spiritual forces must obey. We can say "In the name of Jesus leave" and it will happen.

- **The armor of God**. We can stand firm in His full armor... the helmet of Salvation, breastplate of Righteousness, belt of Truth, readiness from the shoes of the Gospel of Peace, shield Faith, and the sword of the Spirit which is the Word of God (Ephesians 6:10-17).

- **Prayer**. Pray in the Spirit (Ephesians 6:18)! We must fight the battle with God's help in prayer.

- **Praise**. the evil spirit fled from King Saul whenever David praised God using his harp (1 Samuel 16:23). Praising the Lord in song out loud causes the enemy to flee!

SPIRITUAL ATTACK

Am I being attacked by the enemy?
Does the enemy have any foothold in my life?

Below are *six practical steps* to ask Jesus whether you are being attacked by the enemy or not, and if it is for a particular reason:

Step 1
Pray before you begin. Claim the authority of Christ through His shed blood. Command the enemy and any spirits to be silent and not show themselves in Jesus' name. Ask the Lord to speak and that you hear His voice alone.

Step 2
Ask Jesus, "Is there any spirit in my life that needs to be rebuked?" And listen for Him to answer. If "yes," go to Step 3. If "no," thank Jesus for protecting you and move on in your day.

Step 3
Ask Jesus, "Is there any reason for this spirit stay?" Listen for Him to answer. If He answers "yes," go to Step 4. If He answers "no," go to Step 5.

Step 4
Ask Jesus, "What is the reason that this spirit can stay?" And listen for Him to answer. As He answers, you must deal with "the reason" through forgiving others, confessing and repenting of sin, rebuking lies, and renouncing negative generational patterns and ungodly relationships.

Step 5

Proclaim to the spirit, "In the name of Jesus Christ, I command you to leave me and go where Jesus would send you."

Step 6

Ask Jesus, "Is there anything else you want to share with me today?" Listen for His answer.

OTHER HELPFUL RESOURCES

- *Freedom Tools* by Andy Reese and Jennifer Barnett

- *The Strategy of Satan* by Warren W. Wiersbe

- *The Bondage Breaker* and *Victory Over the Darkness* by Neil Anderson

- *Warfare Praying* by Mark Bubeck

YOUR UNIQUE MINISTRY

_____

_____

_____

_____

_____

_____

_____

_____

_____

_____

_____

_____

_____

_____

_____

_____

_____

_____

_____

_____

ENGAGING THE MESSAGE

1. What are your top 2-3 personal takeaways from this message?

_____

_____

_____

_____

_____

_____

_____

2. Did God speak to you in this message in any way? How so?

_____

_____

_____

_____

_____

_____

3. How will these truths change the way you live?

_____

_____

_____

_____

_____

NEXT STEPS

Take some time to fill out the **"Personal Ministry Inventory"** in "The Life Arrow" section of this book.

CORE TAKEAWAYS

- God has uniquely designed every person with a unique ministry in mind! There are no clones or copies. You are a one-of-a-kind original (Psalm 139)!

- God uniquely designed you to do for His special plans and purposes (Eph 2:10)

- God wants to employ your employ your whole life: your talents, spiritual gifts, hobbies, interests, places you show up, past experiences, and even tragedy, pain and suffering to uniquely minister to others.

- You have been given a story to share with others. You don't have to be a Bible scholar to tell others what God has done in your life

As you consider your uniqueness, and how God may desire to use you to naturally connect with others, think about:

- How you enjoy spending your time

- The stage or age of life that you are in

- Your financial resources

- Your positive life experiences (Travel, Job, Relationships, Education, etc.)

- Your difficult life experiences (Sickness/disease/injury, loss of loved ones, loneliness/depression, etc.)

- Spiritual Gifts

- Special Skills

- The unique places you find yourself most commonly (work, school, grocery store, sports fields, neighborhoods, etc.)

Utilizing your unique ministry may mean having to step outside your comfort zone:

- Going outside your normal routine to places you don't normally go.

- Engaging those around you in ways you wouldn't normally engage them.

- Seeking to serve those around you.

EVANGELISM

_____
_____
_____
_____
_____
_____
_____
_____
_____
_____
_____
_____
_____
_____
_____
_____
_____
_____
_____
_____
_____
_____

ENGAGING THE MESSAGE

1. What are your top 2-3 personal takeaways from this message?

_____

_____

_____

_____

_____

_____

_____

2. Did God speak to you in this message in any way? How so?

_____

_____

_____

_____

_____

_____

_____

3. How will these truths change the way you live?

_____

_____

_____

_____

_____

_____

PRAYING FOR THE SPIRITUALLY LOST

- Below, write the names of all the lost people in your life.

- Begin praying for God to open their hearts and minds to His good news.

- Pray for opportunities to share Jesus with them.

- Circle 5 names that you will share with as soon as possible

_____

_____

_____

_____

_____

_____

_____

_____

_____

_____

_____

_____

_____

_____

_____

_____

_____

_____

CORE TAKEAWAYS

- Evangelism means to proclaim the good news.

- We are called to evangelize by God, other believers, the spirit of God in us—and even the lost (their wandering hearts longing for hope) [Mark 16:15; Acts 20:26-27 ; Luke 16:27-28; Matthew 24:46; 1 Corinthians 9:16-17; Acts 16:9; 1 Peter 3:18]

- Both love in-action and in-word is necessary. It is true, Christians are to love in action. But we must proclaim the gospel with our WORDS. Words are always necessary (1 Peter 2:12; 1 Peter 3:15; Romans 10:14-15; Acts 19:8-22).

- Keep it simple! Focus on sharing the good news of Jesus in ways that people can understand and connect with.

- Be willing to share both truth and grace... the reality of God's radical love, and difficult truths to swallow. If we only share hard truths, we miss the love that God has for this world. If we only share about love, we miss the call of God to live lives that honor him.

Additional Evangelism Tips:

- Ask questions, genuinely get to know others and love them. Know their name. Understand what is going on in their life.

- Be opportunistic and initiate: (Col. 4:5) Be aware of opportunities in life: Actively look for people, conversations, and times in which you can share.

- Look for Gospel inroads.

  - What do they need, what struggles do they have, where is there a lack in their life, and what could Jesus do about it?

- Be ready always, be listening for God's prompting. Don't talk yourself out of sharing Jesus with others.

- There is no need to fake being a perfect Christian. Be authentic and genuine. You don't need to bend your convictions for others to "buy in" to your message. They actually want to see true authentic Jesus. Standing by your convictions in a loving way is good and often opens doors for further conversation.

  - Let people ask questions, but know you don't need to know all the answers. You can say:

    "I don't know the answer to that question but I can work on figuring that out with you."

- Share what Jesus is up to in your life! People respond to stories. Often it is these stories of transformation that win people to Jesus more than academic arguments.

- Use spiritual questions and statements to open the door for a conversation:

  - "Where are you on your spiritual journey?"
  - "What do you know about Jesus?"
  - "Who do you think Jesus is?"

OTHER HELPFUL RESOURCES & STRATEGIES

- 4 Spiritual Laws (www.cru.org/how-to-know-god/would-you-like-to-know-god-personally)

- Dare2Share: G.O.S.P.E.L. Acronym (www.dare2share.org/products-resources/free-teen-resources)

- Romans Road (www.biblegateway.-com/blog/2016/09/evangelism- the-romans-road-to-salvation)

- *Miraculous Movements* by Jerry Trousdale: "Discovery Bible Studies" Model (www.thomasnelson.com/miraculous-movements)

- Cru Resources (www.cru.org/train-and-grow/share- the-gospel)

- Evangelism Explosion Resources (evangelismexplosion.org)

- *The Celtic Way of Evangelism* by George Hunter

RESOURCES ON OTHER RELIGIONS

Mormonism

Unveiled Grace: The Story of How We Found Our Way Out of the Mormon Church by Lynn Wilder

Buddhism

Leaving Buddha: A Tibetan Buddhist Monk's Encounter With the Living God by Tenzin Lahkpa and Eugene Bach

Islam

Seeking Allah, Finding Jesus: A Devout Muslim Encounters Christianity by Nabeel Qureshi

No God But One by Nabeel Qureshi

Tribal/Animist

To Every Tribe with Jesus by David Sitton

Hinduism

From Hinduism to Christ by Raj Vemuri

Atheism

The Case For Christ by Lee Strobel

Is Atheism Dead by Eric Metaxas

Jehovah's Witness

The 10 Most Important Things You Can Say to a Jehovah's Witness by Ron Rhodes

APOLOGETICS

ENGAGING THE MESSAGE

1. What are your top 2-3 personal takeaways from this message?

_____
_____
_____
_____
_____
_____
_____

2. Did God speak to you in this message in any way? How so?

_____
_____
_____
_____
_____
_____
_____

3. How will these truths change the way you live?

_____
_____
_____
_____
_____
_____

CORE TAKEAWAYS

Apologetics means "defense of the faith"

2 key questions to evaluate every worldview/religious system:

1. Is the worldview consistent within itself (are there contradictions)?
2. Does it match the reality of the world (fact or fairy- tale)?

A worldview/religion is either THE Way or NO way, it cannot be A way.

Jesus claimed to be God… So, either He was a liar, lunatic, or Lord (He really is who He said He is)

The primary Christian apologetic is the resurrection of Jesus. There is a multitude of evidence to support the fact that Jesus really did rise from the dead. Primarily they revolve around:

- Jesus was a true historical figure and was killed on a Roman cross. Jesus actually lived and died—His death wasn't a magic trick

- Jesus' followers were in despair after his death, but after three days they proclaimed His resurrection in Jerusalem, the very place He died. People would have known if they were telling the truth or proclaiming a lie. If Jesus' followers stole His body and hid it, they would have clearly known it was a lie. They would have known whether His resurrection was a lie or actually true.

- No one dies for a lie that they themselves created, or for something that they know is a lie! Psychology has proven that people will not die for lies; especially torturous deaths for things they know are lies. "Liars make bad martyrs" – Tim Reilly, Atheist turned Evangelist.

- Based on the facts of history, this is the best theory that honest atheists and others have come up with: Jesus' followers must have had hallucinations of a resurrected Jesus.

- But, by definition a hallucination is contained within one person's mind. Not even the best drugs can give an entire group the same hallucination.

- So, the best answer is that Jesus truly rose from the dead, and therefore everything He said matters.

We can have confidence in the Bible:

- The Bible was written over a span of 1500 years by 40 different authors, yet it has one congruent story and theme! That is a miraculous happening!

- There is abundant archeological evidence to support the Biblical story line as historical. In fact, archaeologists often use the Bible to find new digging locations!

- We know from manuscript evidence that the bible has not been corrupted or changed over time. We can confidently say that the words of the Bible (particularly the New Testament) that we have today are the same words that they had in the first years of Christianity.

We can have confidence in that God exists, because he is the most compelling and reasonable explanation for the world around us:

- Life is incredibly complex. The more we discover, the more complex it becomes and the less likely it is that all of it came about by random chance.

- Other theories attempting to explain the origins of life are lacking significant information and are not truly scientific as they cannot be reproduced in a laboratory environment.

- Irreducible Complexity and Watch-Maker Theory

OTHER HELPFUL RESOURCES

- What is "Irreducible Complexity"
  https://www.gotquestions.org/irreducible-complexity.html

- *Reason for God* by Tim Keller

- McDowell Resources
  - www.josh.org/resources/apologetics
  - *Evidence That Demands a Verdict* book
  - *Answers to Tough Questions Skeptics Ask About the Christian Faith* book

- Lee Strobel Ministry
  - www.leestrobel.com
  - *The Case For Christ* book

- Apologetics Messages by RC Sproul
  - www.ligonier.org/learn/series/objections-answered
  - www.ligonier.org/learn/topics/apologetics

THE LOCAL CHURCH

ENGAGING THE MESSAGE

1. What are your top 2-3 personal takeaways from this message?

_____

_____

_____

_____

_____

_____

_____

2. Did God speak to you in this message in any way? How so?

_____

_____

_____

_____

_____

_____

_____

3. How will these truths change the way you live?

_____

_____

_____

_____

_____

_____

CORE TAKEAWAYS

- "Church" most simply means "gathering." It is a gathering of believers in Jesus who come together to worship Him.

- We gather to scatter! Our goal should be mission-minded, gathering together to be equipped to launch back out for every day, everywhere ministry (Ephesians 4:11-12)

- Core elements of a church gathering include: Scriptural teaching, Fellowship with other believers, communion, and prayer (Acts 2:42)

- Each one of us has a role to play and something to offer to build up other believers in the Church (1 Corinthians 14:26)

- Participation in the local church is a crucial aspect of following Jesus (Hebrews 10:25)

- The Church was Jesus' idea and He is the head of it. We make disciples and Jesus builds the Church (Matthew 16:18; Colossians 1:8)

- Rather than criticizing potential "problems" you see in a church setting, work to humbly serve and create potential solutions.

- Use your spiritual gifts to serve the church / other believers (Romans 12:6-8; 1 Corinthians 12:7-11, 28; SpiritualGiftsTest.com)

TIPS FOR FINDING A CHURCH IN YOUR AREA

- The church should be first and foremost focused on Jesus (not primarily on political or social issues).

- The church should be actively engaging God's Word (The Bible).

- The church should be highly focused on engaging God's worldwide mission/the Great Commission (Matthew 28:18-20); including the practices of Acts 2:42

TIPS FOR LAUNCHING A CHURCH IN YOUR REGION

- If a healthy church exists in your area that is characterized by the Biblical qualities above, join what God is up to there!

- If such a church does not exist, prayerfully consider what God would have you do in starting one.

- Make sure the Biblical qualities above are foundational as you consider each new step.

THE VALUE OF ONE: SPIRITUAL MULTIPLICATION

_____
_____
_____
_____
_____
_____
_____
_____
_____
_____
_____
_____
_____
_____
_____
_____
_____
_____
_____
_____
_____
_____

ENGAGING THE MESSAGE

1. What are your top 2-3 personal takeaways from this message?

_____
_____
_____
_____
_____
_____
_____

2. Did God speak to you in this message in any way? How so?

_____
_____
_____
_____
_____
_____
_____

3. How will these truths change the way you live?

_____
_____
_____
_____
_____
_____

CORE TAKEAWAYS

- "More time with less people equals greater Kingdom impact."

- Jesus often ministered to people one life at a time, often through a relational connection

- Jesus impacted individuals around meal tables, on long journeys, in homes, and in other ordinary everyday places and spaces.

- By today's standards, Jesus' ministry could easily look like a failure and be dismissed because it didn't sustain enough early numerical growth. Rather, Jesus spent a lot of time up-close with a relatively small number of disciples – sharing with them His teachings, actions, and life.

- Overtime, relational life-on-life spiritual multiplication is a more powerful way to reach more people than a mass-production program. If we impact someone deeply and then send them to go and do the same, we will multiply (rather than only add), reaching more people over time.

- There is extraordinary value in just one life. And that one is never just one. There are always more lives behind the one. When you impact the one, you may not only be impacting just this one individual, but many others as that individual goes on to impact those they encounter. And those who are impacted by that one individual will still go on to impact others also! By truly impacting one life at a time, we can join Jesus' multiplying movement of Kingdom Laborers (2 Timothy 2:2)!

OTHER HELPFUL RESOURCES

- *Multiplying Movements: A Discipleship Tool For Everyday Followers of Jesus* (Forge)

- *Baton Passing Relationships* booklet by Dwight Robertson (Forge)

- *The Master Plan of Evangelism* by Robert Coleman

- *Training for Trainers* by Ying and Grace Kai

- *Stubborn Perseverance* by James Nyman

RE-ENGAGING LIFE BACK HOME

_____
_____
_____
_____
_____
_____
_____
_____
_____
_____
_____
_____
_____
_____
_____
_____
_____
_____
_____
_____
_____

_____

_____

_____

_____

_____

_____

_____

_____

_____

_____

_____

_____

_____

_____

_____

_____

_____

_____

_____

_____

_____

_____

_____

_____

_____

_____

_____

_____

_____

_____

_____

_____

_____

_____

_____

_____

_____

_____

_____

ENGAGING THE MESSAGE

1. What are your top 2-3 personal takeaways from this message?

_____

_____

_____

_____

_____

_____

_____

2. Did God speak to you in this message in any way? How so?

_____

_____

_____

_____

_____

_____

_____

3. How will these truths change the way you live?

_____

_____

_____

_____

_____

_____

CORE TAKEAWAYS

- Know that you have been on an accelerated journey throughout Forge Equipping. The world at home has remained the same while you have changed.

- When you return home, take on an attitude of humility, not superiority. Think about how you can share your spiritual growth, rather than lord it over others. Seek to love, serve, and impact more than trying to prove who you are or where you are at spiritually.

- Be intentional about keeping-up habits that you have gained during Forge Equipping. Continue to lovingly obey Jesus... staying in your Bible daily, praying and seeking the Lord daily, loving others, and sharing Jesus wherever you go!

- Intimacy with God really is the greatest gift you can give the world. You won't be able to continue moving forward fruitfully if you don't stay intentional in your time with God. Regularly schedule in intentional time with Jesus.

- Be a Kingdom Laborer wherever you go. Love God, Love others, and advance the Kingdom wherever you go.

FORGE EQUIPPING DEBRIEF

50-100 Moments from Forge Equipping

50-100 Moments from Forge Equipping

50-100 Moments from Forge Equipping

BIG 5

Your 5 Most Significant Moments of Forge Equipping

1.

2.

3.

4.

5.

One Word & One Sentence

How would you describe your time at Forge Equipping to a friend or family member in one word? How about in one sentence?

_____

_____

_____

_____

_____

_____

_____

_____

_____

_____

_____

_____

_____

_____

_____

_____

_____

_____

_____

_____

_____

_____

_____

_____

_____

_____

Low Moments

What were three low moments from your time at Forge Equipping?

1.

2.

3.

Lifestyle Change

Was there anything that God revealed to you about yourself that needs to change going forward? Perhaps a particular sin, attitude, or way you function daily that needs to adjust, change, or be removed? Or maybe something you haven't really been engaging that you need to do more of?

_____
_____
_____
_____
_____
_____
_____
_____
_____
_____
_____
_____
_____
_____
_____
_____
_____
_____
_____
_____
_____
_____
_____

Burden Moments

Were there any moments where you sensed God giving you a burden for something He has a burden or desire for?

_____

_____

_____

_____

_____

_____

_____

_____

_____

_____

_____

_____

_____

_____

_____

_____

_____

_____

_____

_____

_____

_____

_____

_____

_____

_____

_____

God Moment(s)

Was there a moment(s) during Forge Equipping that you can look back on as an undeniable moment of God taking action or moving in some way?

_____

_____

_____

_____

_____

_____

_____

_____

_____

_____

_____

_____

_____

_____

_____

_____

_____

_____

_____

_____

_____

_____

_____

Heart Tugs

What do you sense God 'tugging your heart' to do as a result of taking part in Forge Equipping? Are there any specific next steps, action items, ministry objectives, or life changes God is calling you toward?

_____
_____
_____
_____
_____
_____
_____
_____
_____
_____
_____
_____
_____
_____
_____
_____
_____
_____
_____
_____
_____
_____
_____
_____
_____

Paradigm Shift

Were there any moments on Forge Equipping that caused you to have a perspective change? Perhaps you see yourself, others, particular situations, or even the work of the Kingdom differently now?

_____

_____

_____

_____

_____

_____

_____

_____

_____

_____

_____

_____

_____

_____

_____

_____

_____

_____

_____

_____

_____

_____

_____

Anything Else

As you engage this debriefing process, take a moment to ask God if there is anything else He wants to speak to you or remind you of from your time at Forge Equipping...

_____

_____

_____

_____

_____

_____

_____

_____

_____

_____

_____

_____

_____

_____

_____

_____

_____

_____

_____

_____

_____

_____

_____

_____

_____

_____

THE LIFE ARROW

What is the God-given trajectory of your life?

The Life Arrow process will help you unpack what God has been wiring in you, and where your life is going as a result. The Life Arrow will help you fulfill your calling, and may even become a future decision-making grid, keeping you on track with where God is leading.

Burdens

What needs tug most at your heart. Perhaps these are things that make you cry or make you angry; the realities of our world that inspire you to "do something," to take action, to stand up and make a difference.

(These might bring emotion to your core and resonate with you at deep levels; maybe these are areas you would volunteer for; you might really look up to or desire to get up close to others who have this heart or are living out these things; or these might even be prayer themes in your life).

Write out some initial ideas, then move onto "My Heart" on the next page...

_____

_____

_____

_____

_____

_____

_____

_____

_____

_____

_____

_____

_____

_____

_____

_____

_____

_____

MY HEART

What burden has God given me for the world?

Discovering what God has written on our hearts is one of the most difficult things for most to discover and clarity. Wounds, sin, years of status-quo living, boredom, living other's dreams for our lives, fear of failure, and a myriad of other things can silence and put layer upon layer over our hearts.

The following tool is designed to help you begin to peel away these layers and expose what's in your heart. Follow these guidelines that explain the column headings on the heart discovery tool.

HEART PROBES

Consider the categories and questions in the left-hand column (in the chart on the next pages) and reflect and write the specifics in the next column. Because story is a primary language of the human heart, many of the probes focus on stories, movies or other artistic outlets that rouse your heart to life. These probes are designed to help you identify what you prefer and enjoy from different angles of interest. What Bible stories stir the most emotion in you? What Bible characters do you relate to the most? What movies and characters are your all time favorites? What are your favorite sports, art, leaders and heroes? Other probes ask you to identify the specifics about your dreams as a kid, your hopes for the future, what you would do if you knew it wouldn't fail, and what you ultimately care about and how you want to be remembered after you die.

THEMES

When you look at what stirs your heart and why, what themes emerge? Do you see any similar traits or patterns in your answers? Perhaps you discover a heart for the underdog or the most unreached of the world, or the disadvantaged and poor. Or maybe you see a theme for tackling large and seemingly impossible odds. Or perhaps you discover a heart for the marketplace or restoring something gone awry in your industry. Some of the themes may be more general, others specific. That's okay.

MY HEART

Now write one sentence or phrase that captures the essence of the themes you identified. For example, you might discover a heart to teach inner-city youth through sports and after school activities. You might discover your heart to bring your faith into your company through your influence. You might discover a burden to start an initiative that would bring some kind of restorative outcome to your industry. Take time with this statement. It should stir an energy and excitement in you because it is tapping into God's burden He may be placing in you.

MY HEART EXAMPLE
MY HEART'S BURDEN IS FOR THE WORLD

HEART PROBES	SPECIFICS	THEMES	MY HEART
My Favorite Biblical Stories & Characters	• David: His confrontation of Goliath and courageous leadership. • Peter: His passion and risk-taking. • Jesus in the Garden of Gethsemane	A "freedom of the heart" theme.	My heart's burden is to give my love and life freely to my family and friends and to use my talents to help young, disadvantaged entrepreneurs to explore and pursue their dreams and ideas.
My Favorite Movies and Characters	• Braveheart: William Wallace and "Freedom" • Lord of the Rings: Sam Wise Gamgee • It's A Wonderful Life		
My Favorite Sports and/or Art	• Soccer: The "team" and competition of it. • Football: The energy and pace. • Monet: Colors and Setting		
My Favorite Authors/ Writers	• Eldredge: He stirs my heart • Graham: How he weaves faith into fiction • Coelho: The Alchemist and life journey	The need for challenge and adventure in my life.	
My Favorite Leaders	• Winston Churchill: Never, Never Give Up! • Abraham Lincoln: Equality of all. • George W. Bush: Conviction & Freedom theme		
My All Time Heroes	• My dad: perseverance and faithfulness • Jesus: gave up his will for the Father's • William Wallace: Gave the commoners a vision for freedom.	The desire to help other entrepreneurs to optimize their potential and love and serve God, especially the disadvantaged and underprivileged.	
What I Would Do If I Knew I Wouldn't Fail	• Create an international company that would train third world entrepreneurs to start businesses.		
What I Dreamed To Be and Do As A Kid	• To play professional football. • To find the love of my life, travel the world and have a large family.		
What I Hope To Be and Do In My Future	• To have a close, loving family with many grandchildren, to pour my life into younger entrepreneurs and share my faith with them.	To give my love and life freely to my kids and wife.	
What I Ultimately Care About	• Loving those who God has put in my life: my family and friends. • Using my resources and leadership to help young, disadvantaged entrepreneurs to take the risk and have the opportunity to pursue their concepts.		
How I Hope Others Describe Me When I Die	• He kept the big picture in mind. • He used his talents and resources to help those who without an advocate.		

My Heart: My heart's burden for the world

Heart Probes	Specifics	Themes	My Heart
My Favorite Biblical Stories & Characters			
My Favorite Movies & Characters			
My Favorite Sports and/or Arts			
My Favorite Authors/Writers			
My Favorite Leaders			
My All Time Heroes			
What I would Do If I Knew I Wouldn't Fail			
What I Dreamed To Be As A Kid			
What I Hope To Be and Do In My Future			
What I Ultimately Care About			
How I Hope Others Describe Me When I Die			

Mileposts

What major moments altered the direction of your life? What are the mileposts or mile markers—significant events, people, accomplishments, failures, "God moments"—that made you who you are? Use the following pages to capture these mileposts. Run through your life chronologically. Record mileposts and ages when they occurred—as best you can remember.

It may help to ask yourself the following questions as you process:

Q: What relationships have most significantly imprinted your life or shaped your journey?

- Unique friendships
- Special heritage
- Mentor/sponsors
- Complicated or harmful relationships
- Parental oath or commitment
- Seasons when someone came alongside me in a special way

Q: What significant events, experiences or accomplishments have served as building blocks for your journey?

- Giftedness discovery
- Meaningful award or recognition
- Special affirmation or encouragement
- Failures
- Painful or confusing events
- Tragedies

Q: Have you experienced special windows of opportunity or made definitive choices that opened new doors or expanded your horizons?

- Falling forward experiences
- Expanded influence challenges • Life-shaping experiences

Q: Have you had "unexplainable coincidences" or overtly spiritual experiences that shaped your life and/or informed your journey?

- Name significance
- Unusual birth circumstances
- Preservation of life experiences
- Spiritually-based guidance or revelation

_____
_____
_____
_____
_____
_____
_____
_____
_____
_____
_____
_____
_____
_____
_____
_____
_____
_____
_____

Megathemes

Themes are defined as reoccurring ideas. A mega-theme in your life would be a reoccurring idea, pattern, or paradigm that you see happen time and time again. Perhaps there is a word that comes up often for you, or a common pattern of emotions or events. Maybe there are things that people often say about you. Maybe hallmarks of your identity or recurring themes you've seen throughout your entire life.

_____
_____
_____
_____
_____
_____
_____
_____
_____
_____
_____
_____
_____
_____
_____
_____
_____
_____
_____
_____

THEMES FROM FORGE EQUIPPING

*What reoccurring themes did you notice throughout
your time at Forge Equipping?*

_____

_____
_____
_____
_____
_____
_____
_____
_____
_____
_____
_____
_____
_____
_____
_____
_____
_____
_____
_____
_____
_____
_____
_____
_____
_____
_____
_____
_____
_____
_____
_____

Methods

What are your normal "ways" of getting things done?

(Do you work better alone or in a group? Do you research, ask for help from others? Do you 'wing it'? Are you better at understanding the big picture, or dealing with details? Do you prefer to lead and organize, or do you prefer to follow? Make lists? Read? Pray? Consult others? Delegate? Etc.)

Write out some initial ideas, then move onto "Core Talents" on the next page...

_____

_____

_____

_____

_____

_____

_____

_____

_____

_____

_____

_____

_____

_____

_____

_____

_____

_____

_____

CORE TALENTS
What has God gifted me to do?

You have God-given talents. He gave some of them to you when you were born. Some people call these natural talents or abilities. In athletics, we say that a kid has God-given speed or jumping ability or arm strength. In music, we say that a person has a God-given ability to listen to music and then play what he hears. Or we say that someone is a natural leader or natural actor. When we apply discipline, repetition, and practice to our natural talent, we become a master, expert or professional in that area of expression. We all have natural talent, and God is the giver of all of it.

God also gives believers spiritual gifts. Paul says in 1 Corinthians 12:4 that "God's gifts are handed out everywhere; but they all originate in God's Spirit." He doesn't forget anyone. "Each person is given something to do that shows who God is: Everyone gets in on it, everyone benefits. All kinds of things are handed out by the Spirit, and to all kinds of people. The variety is wonderful, wise counsel, clear understanding, simple trust, healing the sick, miraculous acts, proclamation, distinguishing between spirits, tongues, and interpretation of tongues. All these gifts have a common origin but are handed out one by one by the Spirit of God. He decides who gets what, and when" (1 Corinthians 12:7-11, The Message).

Both your natural talents and spiritual gifts come from God. They are his gifts to you. If you are going to fully discover and live your life calling, then you must gain clarity on what gifts and talents he has given you. The following tool will guide you through a process to do so with a series of questions in the left-hand column (in the chart on the next pages).

Passions: What do you love to do? We all love to spend our time and energy doing certain things. What do you love to do so much that when you do it, time speeds up? You can burn hours doing things you love and not realize it. For example, some love to build things, fix things, and learn how things work. Others love the world of thoughts and ideas. They love to read and debate and think about something from all different angles. Others love to compete in sports or the arts. When we are paid to do what we love, work is play. What would you joyfully "suffer" to do? What do you love to do?

Drives: What fuels what you do? Some are driven by results. Others by the process that yields the results. Some are driven by compassion. Others to end world hunger. Some are driven to confront and overcome the impossible or break some kind of human record. Some are driven to contribute to the world in a way that they deem vital and all-important. Others are driven to lead in some way, while others are driven to support and influence those who make primary decisions. What sets you into motion, almost unconsciously? What drives you?

Obsessions: What can't you help but think about? Where does your thinking drift when it is free to do so? When the weight and pressure of the world is off your shoulders, what do you think about? Do you think about restoring, rebuilding, or inventing things? Do you think about helping people? If so, how do you imagine yourself helping them? Do you think about engaging people in some way? If so, what are you doing? And where are you doing it? Oftentimes, we gravitate in our thinking towards zones of activity and contemplation roused by God's giftedness in us. Where does your thinking drift when it is free to do so? What can't you help but think about?

Qualities: How do others describe what you're good at? If I were to ask those who know you best to give me a handful of words that describe you, what would they say? What do you think they would say? And what would they actually say? For example, you may not feel that you have an inquisitive, sharp mind; but other people consistently tell you that they are amazed at how you think. Or other people may have told you that you listen very well or that you have an ability to teach complex concepts in a clear and understandable way. What have others told you over the years that you are good at?

Longings: What must you do or become in your lifetime? As you contemplate the next 2-3 decades of your life, you could do or become a variety of things. There's most likely a few things that rise above all the possibilities. It's these things that would incite the harshest regret if you didn't become or do them. For some, they long to take the risk of launching their entrepreneurial business concept. For others, they long to invest their talent and time to help restore, rebuild, or remedy something broken in their industry or community. What do you long to become or do in your lifetime that if you didn't do it, you'd really regret it?

Expectations: What do you expect from yourself and others? As you engage each day, you expect certain levels of engagement and performance from yourself and from others. For some, they expect to exceed their own expectations and for others to apply their best talent and energy to a project. Others expect to be fully present, to listen well and for others to do the same. Others expect transparent communication and calm under pressure. What do you expect from yourself and from others?

Achievements: What are you glad that you've accomplished? Brag about yourself for a minute. What are you glad that you've done or contributed to that may or may not ever show up on a resume? These things could include projects you've participated in, relationships that you've created, family successes, work related breakthroughs, educational achievements, etc. What thing that you've done do you rejoice about?

After you have reflected deeply and honestly in response to these questions, look for themes in your answers. Write the themes or similar answers in the column to the right (in the chart on the next pages). And then summarize these themes in the "My Core Talents" column. See the Next page for an example.

Brainstorm Space:

_____
_____
_____
_____
_____
_____
_____
_____
_____
_____
_____
_____
_____
_____
_____
_____
_____
_____
_____
_____
_____
_____
_____
_____
_____
_____
_____

Key Questions	Details	Themes	Core Talents
Passions What do I love to do?	Learn about history, be in nature, business, invest in God's kingdom, design, build		**Entrepreneurial Creator:** I have the ability to find new investment opportunities with high-yield return on investments
Drives What fuels what I do?	Discovering new opportunities, bring ideas to life, lead teams, accomplish the impossible	I am good at strategy and identifying new opportunities	
Obsessions What do I constantly think about?	Find good investments, negotiate good deals, build trust, build team, world economy, best business practices		
Qualities How do others describe what I'm good at?	Good with people, savvy businessman, clear communication, strategic thinker, trustworthy	I am an effective team leader	**Communicator:** I have a gift to teach complex concepts in clear, compelling deliveries
Longings What must I do or become in my life?	Be faithful and balanced in my life, be engaged in relationships, take risks to pursue entrepreneurial drive, help bring entrepreneurial thinking and growth to impoverished, under educated parts of the world	I am a clear communicator	**Primary Leader** I am gifted to lead teams and have the experience to do so
Expectations What do I expect from myself and from others?	Full engagement, team collaboration and hearing various perspectives, justice – doing the right thing and brining justice to things that are unjust	I have a gift to find strong returns on investments	
Achievements What am I glad that I've accomplished?	Helped church save thousands of dollars, led mission trip to Brazil, helped 85-yr old neighbor get her furnace fixed, teaching next level leadership to a sister company	I am good at fixing things with my hands and figuring out how to do so	**Builder:** I have the skill to build and fix things, and can do so by leading a project or doing it myself

My Core Talents: What has God gifted me to do?

Key ?s	Details	Themes	Core Talents
Passions What do I love to do?			
Drives What fuels what I do?			
Obsessions What do I constantly think about?			
Qualities How do others describe what I'm good at?			
Longings What must I do or become in my life?			
Expectations What do I expect from myself and from others?			
Achievements What am I glad that I've accomplished?			

Dreams

What are your aspirations or ideas that could become a God-given clarified vision in the future? What would you love to do, be, or see happen?

_____

_____

_____

_____

_____

_____

_____

_____

_____

_____

_____

_____

_____

_____

_____

_____

_____

_____

_____

_____

_____

_____

_____

_____

DREAMING FOR YOUR LIFE

Your God-Given Direction/Identity

Judges 6 (Take note of verse 12)

Gideon was hiding in a wine press, yet God still called Gideon a *mighty warrior*. It was who God saw Gideon as and who God was calling Gideon to be.

Who is God calling you to become?

"Dreaming begins with listening." –Steve Moore

Dreaming for Your Life Exercise:

1. Spend the next 20–30 minutes in a prayer posture quietly listening for God's voice for. Ask God what He thinks of you. Ask Him to reveal His dreams for your life to you, keeping in mind that He may reveal something you have not even considered. Be open. Release any fear to Him.

2. On the next page, write down bits and pieces of thoughts, ideas or mental pictures that come to mind.

3. Based on all God has been revealing, prayerfully think through a 2-word name like Gideon's: a Descriptive Word and an Identity Word (Like Gideon being called "Mighty Warrior")

DREAMING FOR OTHERS

"Dreaming begins with listening." —Steve Moore

Dreaming for Others Exercise:

1. Spend time with God in a prayer posture quietly listening for God's voice for each person in your fellowship. Ask God what He thinks of them and what He has for you to share with them. Ask Him to reveal His dreams for their life to you, keeping in mind that He may reveal something you have not even considered. Be open. Release any fear to Him. Write down what you hear for each person on a separate sheet of paper (We recommend 1 piece of paper per person)

2. Use one blank page for each person in your fellowship: Write their name at the top. Then as you pray, write down bits and pieces of thoughts, ideas or mental pictures that come to mind as they pertain to your teammates.

3. This is not a time to encourage your teammates with what you like about them, what you think, or what you see. This is a time to let God share what HE thinks.

Below, take notes of what others on the team share with you:

_____
_____
_____
_____
_____
_____
_____
_____

Mission

Why do you exist? Why did God give you to the world? The goal is to write out the central purpose of your life in one simple sentence. Remember this is *your* mission. This mission should be unique to you.

Start off by writing out key emphasis words that resonate with your heart. Make sure to go back through every portion of "Forge Equipping Debrief" and "The Life Arrow" that you have completed up to this point and look for repeated words. Write those words here as well.

_____

_____

_____

_____

_____

_____

_____

_____

_____

_____

_____

_____

_____

_____

_____

_____

_____

_____

_____

_____

MY MISSION STATEMENT

After writing down all these key words, circle your top 3-5 words.

Then begin to craft a mission statement using these words, pointing it in the direction that God has been leading you! Consider what has been revealed up to this point (including the dreams category).

Use the space below to brainstorm and work on it.

Utilize this structure for your mission statement:
"I exist to... _____ so that... _____"

_____
_____
_____
_____
_____
_____
_____
_____
_____
_____
_____
_____
_____
_____
_____
_____
_____
_____
_____
_____
_____
_____
_____

Vision

Describe in detail the results of accomplishing your life mission (from the last section). What do you see as the ultimate impact of your life as if you are at the end looking back on the life you have lived (seeing your contribution from the other end of your life)? Build out from the "so that" portion of your mission statement.

Start your vision statements with "I see…"

_____

_____

_____

_____

_____

_____

_____

_____

_____

_____

_____

_____

_____

_____

_____

_____

_____

_____

_____

_____

_____

Resources

What specific resources are "in your hand" to help you accomplish your mission? Perhaps there are specific people or relationships, property, technology, gifts, and talents God has given you, or even other monetary resources that you have unique access to and can leverage for the sake of the mission God has given you...

_____

_____

_____

_____

_____

_____

_____

_____

_____

_____

_____

_____

_____

_____

_____

_____

_____

_____

_____

_____

_____

_____

_____

SPIRITUAL GIFTS

Your spiritual gifts are a God-given resource to help accomplish your God-God-given mission...

1. Take a look at your spiritual gifts test results.

2. Read the following passages:

    Romans 12: 6-8
    1 Corinthians 12: 8-11
    Ephesians 4:11-13

3. After looking at your test results and reading all of the above passages, pray, listen, and write down what you believe are your top spiritual gifts:

_____

_____

_____

_____

_____

_____

_____

_____

_____

_____

_____

_____

_____

_____

_____

_____

_____

_____

PERSONAL MINISTRY INVENTORY

Do a quick inventory of the things in your life that God can employ to impact the world...

> One of the greatest joys in life comes when we live out God's purpose for us. He has designed each of us like no other and His design is perfect for Kingdom impact. Perhaps that's why God seems to give us the entrepreneurial freedom to creatively apply our gifts and passions to advance His Kingdom.

> What could every day impact look like if it is as distinct and unique as you are? We invite you to do an inventory of the things in your life that God can employ. It could help you discover more about how God can employ *who you are* to minister to others *where they are*.

What Does Ministry Look Like?

> Often, we have a tendency to believe that to be in ministry, we must be a pastor, missionary, musician or some other "typical" ministry vocation.

> But that's just not the case. God has created each of us uniquely to carry out the distinct ministry He's called us to. We can use our gifts, passions, hobbies, and interests for the Kingdom. What is unique about you that can be used for the Kingdom?

What are your hobbies and/or recreational interests?

☐ Fly Fishing
☐ Cooking/Baking
☐ Running/Working out
☐ Skateboarding
☐ Gardening or Lawn Work
☐ Investing
☐ Traveling
☐ Motorcycling/Bicycling
☐ Knitting/Sewing
☐ Painting
☐ _____
☐ _____

What unique roles do you hold, or what season of life are you in?

☐ Student
☐ Single
☐ Professional
☐ Early Married
☐ Parents of Young Children
☐ Parents of Teenagers
☐ Empty Nester
☐ Retired
☐ Grandparent
☐ Part of a Bowling League
☐ Teacher
☐ _____
☐ _____

What are your tangible and financial resources?

- ☐ Guest Room
- ☐ Extra Vehicle/Ability to Drive Others
- ☐ Camping or Adventure Gear
- ☐ Reward Points/Frequent Flyer Miles
- ☐ Tools and Equipment/A Lawn Mower
- ☐ Legacy Giving
- ☐ Stock Giving
- ☐ Savings
- ☐ _____
- ☐ _____

What are some life experiences you have had?

- ☐ Travel Experiences
- ☐ Job Experiences
- ☐ Relationship Experiences
- ☐ Educational Experiences
- ☐ _____
- ☐ _____

What are some painful life experiences you have had?

- ☐ Cancer Survivor
- ☐ Loss of a Child or Other Family Member
- ☐ Injury
- ☐ Spiritual Struggle
- ☐ Dark-Night of the Soul
- ☐ Loneliness
- ☐ _____

Do you have any special skills?

☐ Mechanical
☐ Hospitality
☐ Art
☐ Music
☐ Carpentry
☐ Writing
☐ _____
☐ _____

Where and When Does Ministry Happen?

Think about it for a second... ministry happens in the ordinary venues of life. Not only at church, a Christian conference or retreat, or on a short-term mission trip.

Here are some examples:

☐ With our families
☐ At our church
☐ At work
☐ In our neighborhoods
☐ At events
☐ At block parties
☐ With our neighbors and their interests
☐ At school
☐ In a dorm
☐ At our lockers
☐ In our classes
☐ At the Student Union
☐ In our communities
☐ In our clubs
☐ In our civic organizations
☐ At Parent-Teacher organizations
☐ With our boards
☐ At rescue missions
☐ At ministry organizations
☐ Along the way
☐ In the grocery store
☐ At a restaurant
☐ At the bank
☐ At the gas station
☐ At the post office

Where are the ordinary venues in your life?

Objectives

What do you want to accomplish in each area of your life going forward? These areas may include: spiritual life, daily mission, family, school or job, physical, financial, social, etc.

_____
_____
_____
_____
_____
_____
_____
_____
_____
_____
_____
_____
_____
_____
_____
_____
_____
_____
_____
_____
_____
_____
_____
_____
_____

PEOPLE

Are there any specific people God is asking you to intentionally reach out to (friends, family, school friends, coworkers)? Who are they? What is God asking you to do?

_____

_____

_____

_____

_____

_____

_____

_____

_____

_____

_____

_____

_____

_____

_____

_____

_____

_____

_____

_____

_____

_____

_____

_____

_____

_____

_____

_____

LOST PEOPLE TO ENGAGE

Who in your life does not know Jesus? Below, write the names of everyone you can think of in your life who does not know Jesus. Circle the first five that you sense God calling you to engage.

_____

_____

_____

_____

_____

_____

_____

_____

_____

_____

_____

_____

_____

_____

_____

_____

_____

_____

_____

_____

_____

_____

_____

_____

_____

BELIEVERS TO EQUIP AS LABORERS

In the space bellow write a list of people who you could help grow and equip in their spiritual life using Multiplying Movements.

Next Steps

Write out the goals you have as an extension of your mission.

Please use the next several pages to detail your goals
in each of the categories below:

LIFE-TIME GOALS

What do you want to see happen in your lifetime?

_____
_____
_____
_____
_____
_____
_____
_____
_____
_____
_____
_____
_____
_____
_____
_____
_____
_____
_____

MID-RANGE GOALS

What do you want to see in the next 3-5 years?

_____

_____

_____

_____

_____

_____

_____

_____

_____

_____

_____

_____

_____

_____

_____

_____

_____

_____

_____

_____

_____

_____

_____

_____

_____

_____

_____

_____

_____

_____

_____

_____

FIRST YEAR GOALS

What do you want to see in the next 90 days to 1 year?

_____

_____

_____

_____

_____

_____

_____

_____

_____

_____

_____

_____

_____

_____

_____

_____

_____

_____

_____

_____

_____

_____

_____

_____

_____

_____

_____

_____

_____

_____

IMMEDIATE NEXT STEPS

What are the very next steps you will take as soon as you are home?

_____

_____

_____

_____

_____

_____

_____

_____

_____

_____

_____

_____

_____

_____

_____

_____

_____

_____

_____

_____

_____

_____

_____

_____

_____

_____

_____

_____

OBSTACLES

What 3-5 things will get in the way of you daily living out your mission and vision in both your immediate arm long-term next steps?

_____
_____
_____
_____
_____
_____
_____
_____
_____
_____
_____
_____
_____
_____
_____
_____
_____
_____
_____
_____
_____
_____
_____
_____
_____
_____
_____

HELPS

What 3-5 things will get in the way of you daily living out your mission and vision in both your immediate arm long-term next steps?

_____
_____
_____
_____
_____
_____
_____
_____
_____
_____
_____
_____
_____
_____
_____
_____
_____
_____
_____
_____
_____
_____
_____
_____
_____
_____
_____
_____

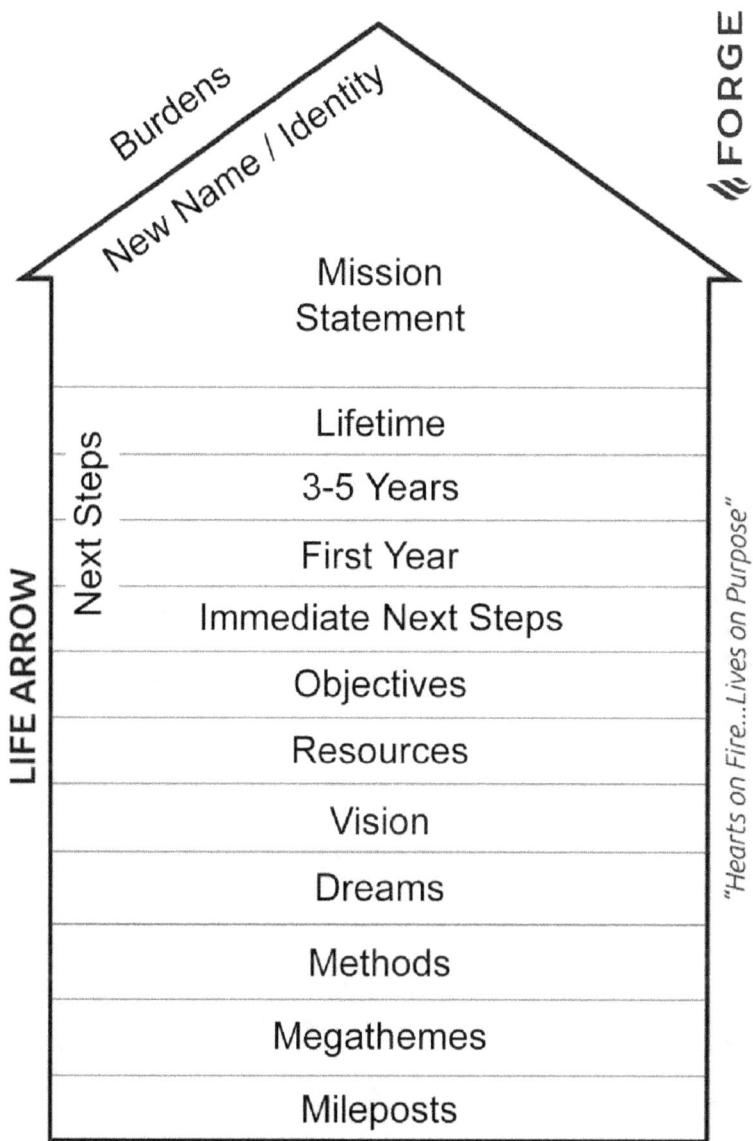

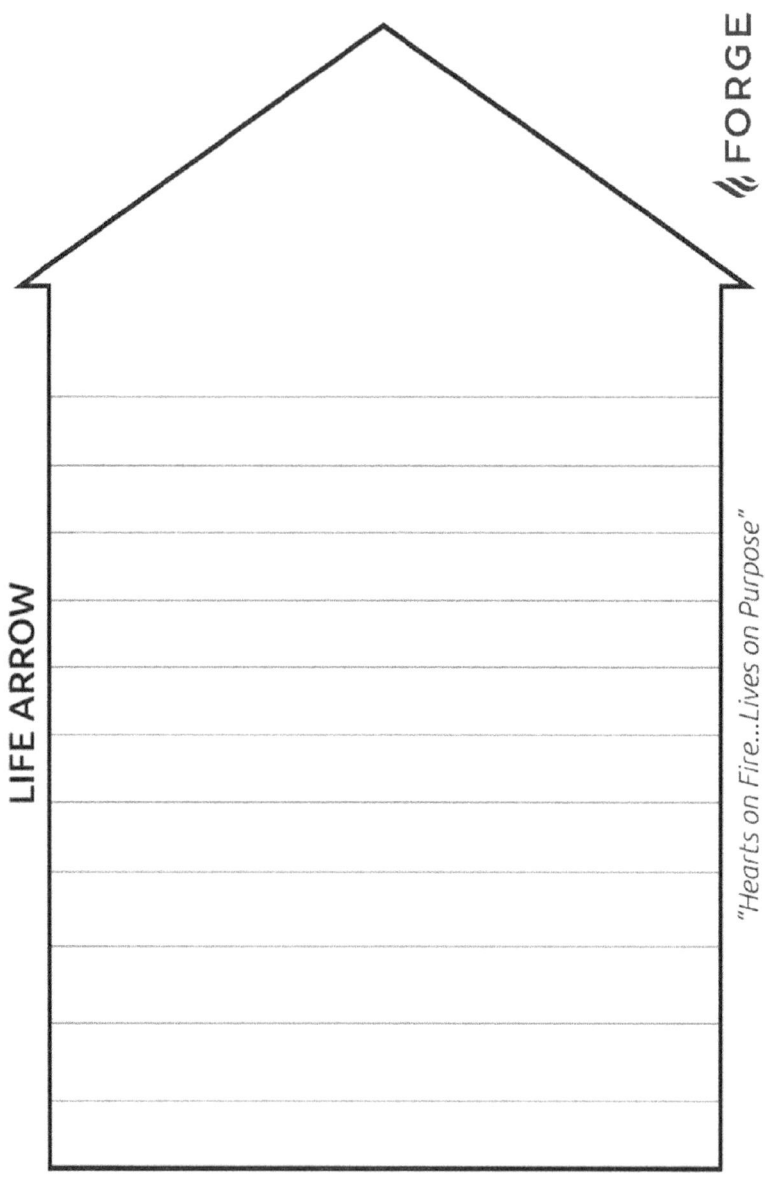

LIFE ARROW

FORGE

"Hearts on Fire...Lives on Purpose"

BECOMING AN EFFECTIVE KINGDOM LABORER

As part of your training through Forge, you are being launched out with a personal 3-prong vision of impact, starting when you get home.

This is an invitation to become a 24/7/365 Kingdom Laborer with a ministry as unique as you are, as a lifestyle.

As you have wrapped up the life arrow process, fill in the following for your 3-pronged vision that God is launching you into:

YOUR UNIQUE MINISTRY VISION

How will you utilize your God-given uniqueness to impact others and engage those who do not yet know Jesus?

_____

_____

_____

_____

YOUR MULTIPLYING MOVEMENTS VISION

How will you incorporate the practice of spiritual multiplication and tool of Multiplying Movements into your life? Who will you begin with?

_____
_____
_____
_____
_____
_____
_____
_____
_____
_____
_____
_____
_____
_____
_____
_____
_____
_____
_____
_____
_____
_____
_____
_____
_____
_____
_____
_____

YOUR LOCAL CHURCH VISION

How will you use your spiritual gifts and abilities to serve your church?

_____
_____
_____
_____
_____
_____
_____
_____
_____
_____
_____
_____
_____
_____
_____
_____
_____
_____
_____
_____
_____
_____
_____
_____
_____
_____
_____

YOUR ONGOING IMPACT

The greatest gift you will ever give the world is your intimacy with God. Without this, your impact will be diminished.

So, how will you specifically maintain an up-close relationship with Jesus going forward?

_____

_____

_____

_____

_____

_____

_____

_____

_____

_____

_____

_____

_____

_____

_____

_____

_____

_____

_____

_____

_____

_____

_____

_____

_____

_____

_____

_____

NOTES

NOTES

MORE FORGE RESOURCES & OPPORTUNITIES

FORGE SPEAKERS & EVENTS
ForgeSpeakers.org

Need someone to challenge your group to become passionate followers of Jesus who live with hearts on fire and lives on purpose? Book a Forge speaker for your next event!

FORGE EQUIPPING PROGRAMS for ALL AGES
ForgeTraining.org

Forge Equipping is not summer camp and training events "as usual." Forge challenges and equips people of all ages to become unique, lifelong Kingdom laborers every day, everywhere.

FORGE BOOKS & RESOURCES
ForgeResources.org

Looking for a deeper relationship with God and practical ways to widen His Kingdom impact through your life? Forge has the resources you need.

THE FORGE APP
Essential Kingdom Laboring tools right at your fingertips:
TheForgeApp.org

JOIN THE MULTIPLYING MOVEMENT
Where everyday followers become Kingdom multipliers:
MultiplyingMovements.com

FORGE VIDEO CONTENT
Subscribe to free video content:
Youtube.com/ForgeForward

FORGE PODCAST
FuelForTheHarvest.com

FORGE DAILY TEXTS
Scan the QR code or visit ForgeForward.org/Sparks
to join Spark of the Day
for one-sentence daily devotionals.

NEED PRAYER?
Email us at Prayer@ForgeForward.org

CONTACT US
14485 E. Evans Avenue
Denver, Colorado 80014
303.745.8191
info@forgefoward.org

Learn more and get involved at
ForgeForward.org

www.ingramcontent.com/pod-product-compliance
Lightning Source LLC
Chambersburg PA
CBHW071145130626
46553CB00004B/1526